GREEN CUISINE

THE GUARDIAN'S

Selection of the Best Vegetarian Recipes

Other titles by Colin Spencer
CORDON VERT
MEDITERRANEAN VEGETARIAN COOKING

GREEN CUISINE

—— THE GUARDIAN'S ——
Selection of the Best Vegetarian Recipes

Selected and Introduced by Colin Spencer

Recipes tested by Jane Harrington and Sess Merrison
for Leith's School of Food and Wine

THORSONS PUBLISHING GROUP
Wellingborough, Northamptonshire
·
Rochester, Vermont

First published 1986

British Library Cataloguing in Publication Data

Green cuisine: the Guardian's selection of the
  best vegetarian recipes.
  1. Vegetarian cookery
  I. Spencer, Colin   II. The Guardian
  641.5'636   TX837

ISBN 0-7225-1268-6

Printed and bound in Italy

CONTENTS

FOREWORD

AMONG all the changes that have overtaken British taste and consumption in the lifetime of the middle-aged, the greening of our cuisine is one of the least expected — and most welcome, even if you do not happen to share the assumptions on which it is based. And the ferment continues. No one knows better than the editor of the *Guardian*'s Food and Drink page how many ideas bubble up when cooks with minds of their own get together as they did during the 1985 competition that has happily led to this book. Knowing this, I half-expected the quality of the winners' work to surprise conventional caterers. But the results still took me aback.

One surprise was the finalists' rejection of the 'vegetarian' label. In other words, the best recipes and best-balanced menus, in the opinion of professional judges, tended to come from people who had no doctrinal chopper to hone but who had found for themselves, in the despised roots and greens and pulses of former times, an unexplored range of food harmonies, waiting to be revealed by a skilled (if usually self-taught) master or mistress of kitchen craft. This promises well for the future, especially perhaps where actual vegetarians have until recently been almost universally neglected: that is, in restaurants.

My other surprise was the subtlety of the marriages between food and wine achieved by some (not all) competitors. Here, altogether new ground is being broken, for the food culture of our chief European wine-producing countries depends heavily on meat and fish. In Britain, where popular experience of wine in all its global variety is still only beginning, we may be readier to experiment in matching wine to different kinds of food. But it is still remarkable how far we have travelled in a short time from the steak-and-Liebfraumilch ads of a few years back. I hope readers of this book will not try too hard to repeat the writers' own wine choices — though a honeyed Barsac with two-year-old Gouda cheese was an experience I would happily meet again. It is sufficient to have the point made that if it is worth a host or hostess giving time and thought and expense to food, the same is true of drink — and vice versa. And as yet, with green cuisine, there are no rules to inhibit you. *Bon appetit.*

CHRISTOPHER DRIVER

INTRODUCTION

IN THE last dozen years, vegetarian cooking has struggled to come out of the Dark Age. This book signals the dawn of the Renaissance. Early last year, we said in the *Guardian* that the 'Greens' had come to power in the modern kitchen and we set some rigorous rules for the 1985 Guardian Cookery Competition. It was sponsored by Gazela Wines and Leith's School of Food and Wine and we hoped that it would be a challenge to all creative cooks whether they were vegetarian or not. We were astonished at the quality of the response.

Competitors had to be over eighteen and have nothing to do with *Guardian* Newspapers Limited, Prudence Leith Limited, Gazela Wines Limited, David Russell PR Consultants Limited, or any subsidiaries. We made it clear that, when we said vegetarian, we meant lacto-vegetarian, so that dairy produce and eggs were permitted, but we did also say that we would be strict in that no gelatine or chicken stock cubes would be allowed. We slipped up once because we forgot about animal rennet in cheese and some competitors chose vegetarian cheeses while others did not. As this was our fault, we did not allow the issue to sway us in the final choice.

Competitors were asked for a first course, then a main course of two contrasting dishes, then a salad conceived as both a pause in the meal and a bridge towards the choice of three different cheeses. The meal was to end with a pudding, either hot or cold. The first and main courses had to match Gazela's white Vinho Verde and red Dão Grão Vasco but we then asked the competitors to choose another wine from any region in the world to accompany the cheeses, the pudding, or both. All we specified was that that wine had to cost under £10 a bottle and be obtainable in British shops. The amounts of the meal had to be planned for four people. At the first stage, we did not require detailed recipes. That would come later when the six finalists chosen, but we did ask for details of the method of cooking.

We touched on the vexed question of plagiarism for we know too well that few recipes are wholly original. So we said that no competitor would be penalized for minor borrowings, but that we would like debts to be acknowledged.

The first prize was a trip for two to Portugal in September, staying for three days in the medieval Azevedo Castle. This was the home of Gazela Wines and had been handsomely restored by them. As it happened, the restoration was unfinished so the winners stayed in a hotel in Oporto and paid a visit to the castle. The second prize was one month's intensive, advanced cookery course at Leith's School. Both the winners also received a case each of Gazela Vinho Verde and Dão Grão Vasco. The third prize was four cases of these wines. Other finalists also received wine and a *Guardian* voucher for £20 worth of books on food or wine to spend at Books for Cooks which the owner, Heidi Lascelles, generously made up to £25. The judges were Prue Leith, David Russell, Aileen Hall, Christopher Driver and myself.

We had over 130 entries from all over Britain and they showed an enterprising range of imaginative recipes which this book reflects. In these pages, you will find the whole menus of the six finalists, including the last in the book which is by Lynn Walford who sadly could not make the Cook-In on July 18th. The rest of the book contains a personal choice of the best recipes and sounds the death knell of the nut cutlet or nut roast. On the night of the Cook-In, the tutors at Leith's were amazed at the quality of the food. It was a revelation to them that vegetarian cooking could be so light and look so appealing. It was also astonishing to me that the five finalists could cook this complicated meal from scratch in two and a half hours but they did it magnificently and the judges had a harrowing job in choosing the winner. The most popular dish of the evening was Caroline Stay's Spinach and Lemon Mousselines with Avocado (page 40). But the more the judges toured and tasted, the more we disagreed among ourselves. Some of us found Jill Robinson's Tomato and Basil Sauce (page 16) refreshing while others found it too sharp. I loved Miranda Kennett's Roquefort Sauce with the Melon (page 86) while Aileen Hall, who was our wine authority that evening, found it too strong. When it came to the judges' decision, we all fought for our favourites and were only controlled by Prue Leith playing at headmistress. Marks out of ten were given for each course; then for how apt the matching of the wines were; and a third mark was given for the overall concept of the meal.

I accompanied Jill Robinson and her husband to Portugal and

I was impressed at the trouble she had taken in deciding on the winning menu. She had planned variations on the meal for weeks ahead and invited friends and family to taste and judge the various flavours. If anyone deserved to win, I felt she did.

On the evening of the judging, there was a common consensus that vegetarian food as enchanting as this could not have been created ten years ago. This we believed was true cordon vert and the green cuisine revolution was well on its way.

The recipes in this book are often bold, like M. van der Veen's Red Wine and Lentil Soup (page 25), or delicate like Mrs Jackson's Mangetout Soup (page 27), and what a delicious idea for summer is Helen Clipsom's Iced Herb Soup (page 23). The ideas also come from all over the world.

In this selection, I have deviated slightly from the plan by calling some dishes 'main' while others are 'side'. In the competition, the main course was made up of two contrasting dishes. But quite often, one of them appeared to be more substantial than the other. A gâteau of crêpes, tarts, stuffed pancakes, a saffron gougère and various pastas are all put in this section, with original sauces and methods of cooking. The salads too are far from the concept of a few lettuce leaves mixed with cucumber and tomato. The salads here show a delicious range of ideas from nasturtium flowers, fruit salads and ones with the rarer leaf vegetables like escarole and Italian chicories. I make no apology for choosing four raspberry puddings out of the fifteen. It was, after all, July when the contestants had to cook and all their menus reflected the produce of the season. I also think that these four recipes with raspberries are all intriguingly new.

The judges at the *Guardian* expected this competition to help take vegetarian food in Britain out of the leaden gloom of the nut roast and the statutory omelette into a new era of freshness and lightness, of simple and striking flavours and combinations. I think this book proves overwhelmingly that our expectations were right.

COLIN SPENCER

WINNING MENU

Jill Robinson

(Illustrated overleaf.)

FIRST COURSE
Courgette and Leek Timbales with Fresh Tomato and Basil Sauce
WINE: Gazela Vinho Verde

MAIN COURSE
Ribbon Cake
WINE: Gazela Dão Grão Vasco

SIDE DISH
Noodles and Vegetables served with a Walnut and Tahini Sauce

SALAD
Wheatberry Salad

CHEESES
Caerphilly, Chewton Mendip Cheddar, Shropshire Blue, served with Oatcakes and Radishes
WINE: Vouvray - Château Moncontour 1983

PUDDING
Red Fruit Tartlets
WINE: Vouvray - Château Moncontour 1983

Courgette and Leek Timbales with Fresh Tomato and Basil Sauce

For the timbales:
A little vegetable oil
8 oz (225g) courgettes
8 oz (225g) small leeks
1 oz (25g) butter
¼ pint (150ml) Greek sheep's
    yogurt
1 tablespoon plain flour
Sea salt
Freshly ground black pepper

For the sauce:
1 lb (450g) fresh ripe tomatoes
Fresh basil, to taste
2 tablespoons tomato purée
Juice of 1 lemon
Sea salt
Freshly ground black pepper
Pinch sugar
Olive oil (about 5 tablespoons)

FIRST, PREPARE the timbales. Lightly oil 4 ramekins. Thinly slice 1 courgette and blanch for 2 minutes in boiling water, then drain, refresh in cold water, and drain again. Line the ramekins with the slices.

Clean and chop the rest of the courgettes and the leeks. Heat the butter in a pan and stew the vegetables with 3 tablespoons water for 5 minutes. Liquidize or process.

Place the yogurt in a bowl and beat in the flour, then stir in the vegetable purée. Season to taste. Fill the ramekins, place in a bain marie and bake at 350°F/180°C (Gas Mark 4) for 20 minutes. Leave to cool.

To make the sauce, process the tomatoes, then sieve to obtain a smooth purée. Process again with the basil, tomato purée, lemon juice to taste, salt, pepper and sugar. Finally, pour some olive oil down the feeder tube, while the machine is running, to enrich and smooth the sauce.

Pour a little sauce onto each plate and unmould a timbale in the centre. Decorate with extra basil leaves.

For the omelettes:
6 eggs, beaten
1 bunch parsley, finely
   chopped
Sea salt
Freshly ground black pepper
1 tablespoon cold water

For the mushroom filling:
6 oz (150g) mushrooms
1 oz (25g) butter
4 fl oz (120ml) Dão Grão Vasco
   wine
1 oz (25g) flour and butter,
   kneaded
Sea salt
Freshly ground black pepper

For the spinach filling:
12 oz (350g) spinach
1 oz (25g) butter
1 oz (25g) flour
¼ pint (150ml) milk
4 oz (100g) Stilton cheese
Sea salt
Freshly ground black pepper

For the aubergine filling:
1 medium aubergine
Sea salt
Olive oil, for frying
2 shallots, finely chopped
8 oz (225g) tomatoes, skinned,
   seeded and chopped
Freshly ground black pepper

1 tablespoon Parmesan cheese,
   for topping
1 tablespoon wholemeal
   breadcrumbs, for topping

Ribbon Cake

BEAT TOGETHER the ingredients for the omelettes. Make 4 thin omelettes and set aside.

For the first filling, slice the mushrooms and sweat in the butter. After 1 minute, pour in the wine and simmer briefly. Remove the mushrooms with a slotted spoon before thickening with kneaded butter. Season to taste. Return the mushrooms to the pan, remove from the heat and reserve.

For the second filling, wash the spinach and strip away the stems. Cook for 3 minutes in just the water that clings to the leaves. Drain well, squeezing out any excess liquid. Chop roughly. Heat the butter in a pan, use the flour to make a roux, then make a sauce with the milk and cheese. Stir in the spinach, season to taste and set aside.

For the third filling, slice the aubergine finely then sprinkle with salt and leave for the bitter juices to be drawn out. Wash well and drain. Heat 2 tablespoons of oil in a pan and sauté the aubergine slices for 5 minutes, then add the shallots and tomatoes. Simmer for at least 15 minutes, stirring frequently. Season to taste.

To assemble the dish, build up layers of omelettes and sauces, sprinkling the top omelette with a mixture of Parmesan and breadcrumbs. Place in the oven at 325°F/170°C (Gas Mark 3) for 15 minutes to warm through.

Noodles and Vegetables served with a Walnut and Tahini Sauce

For the sauce:
4 oz (100g) walnuts
1 clove garlic, chopped
4 fl oz (120ml) tahini
Juice of 1 lemon
4 fl oz (120ml) water
Sea salt
Freshly ground black pepper

For the noodles and vegetables:
4 oz (100g) dwarf French beans
4 oz (100g) mangetout peas
1 bulb fennel
1 bunch new carrots
8 oz (225g) fresh white noodles
1 oz (25g) butter
Sea salt
Freshly ground black pepper
Toasted sesame seeds

PLACE THE walnuts and garlic in a blender or processor and process until smooth. Add all the other sauce ingredients and process briefly, adding more water if necessary.

Trim the beans and peas, slice the fennel and carrots into julienne strips, and steam all the vegetables for 5 minutes. Cook the noodles in plenty of boiling salted water for 4 minutes. Drain and keep warm.

To serve, dress the noodles with the sauce, toss the vegetables with the butter and a little seasoning, then fold the two mixtures gently in together. Scatter with toasted sesame seeds and serve.

Wheat Berry Salad

4 oz (100g) wheat berries
1 red pepper
1 yellow pepper
2 courgettes
2 oz (50g) mushrooms
1 bunch spring onions
Soya sauce
Red wine vinegar
Sea salt
Freshly ground black pepper
1 hearty cos lettuce

SOAK THE wheat berries for 30 minutes, then drain, place in a pan with fresh water, and cook for 1 hour. Drain and cool. Chop the peppers and courgettes finely. Slice the mushrooms and slice the onions diagonally. Toss with the wheat berries and dress with soya sauce, wine vinegar and seasoning.

On a flat dish, spread cos lettuce leaves in a circle. Place the salad in the centre so that leaves can be used as scoops if wished.

½ oz (15g) sunflower
    margarine
Scant ¼ pint (140ml) hot
    water
8 oz (225g) fine oatmeal
¼ teaspoon bicarbonate of
    soda
½ teaspoon salt

Oatcakes

MELT THE margarine in the hot water. Place the oatmeal in a bowl with the bicarbonate of soda and the salt. Pour in the liquid and use a palette knife to mix to a moist dough.

Dust the surface of a slab with extra oatmeal and roll out the dough as thinly as possible. Use a round cutter to make the oatcakes and place them on an ungreased baking sheet. Cook at 350°F/180°C (Gas Mark 4) for about 20 minutes, until golden, turning once during cooking. Cool on a rack and offer with the cheese course.

Red Fruit Tartlets

For the rich pastry:
6 oz (150g) plain flour
3 oz (75g) softened butter
1 egg yolk
Juice of 1 lemon
1 tablespoon icing sugar
Sea salt

For the filling:
1 pot fromage blanc (approx.
    12 fl oz/450ml)
Icing sugar to taste
8 oz (225g) raspberries
8 oz (225g) hulled strawberries
8 oz (225g) trimmed
    redcurrants
8 oz (225g) cherries, stoned
Redcurrant jelly, to glaze

MAKE THE pastry in a food processor, amalgamate into a ball, and chill for at least 30 minutes. Then roll out thinly and line 12 small tartlet tins. Prick the bases and place a small ball of crumpled foil in each. Place the tins on a baking tray and cook at 400°F/200°C (Gas Mark 6) for about 10 minutes, without allowing to burn at the edges. Remove from the oven, remove the foil, and return to the oven for a few more minutes to finish cooking. Remove from the tins and cool.

Place the fromage blanc in a bowl and fold in icing sugar to taste. Spoon a little into the base of each tart. Decorate with the fruits — either three tartlets of each sort, or a selection of fruit on each, but leave the centres clear for a contrast of colour. Melt the redcurrant jelly with a little water and glaze the fruits. Place three tartlets on each plate, and garnish with a few of the fruits you will have left over.

SOUPS AND STARTERS

Iced Herb Soup

1 lb (450g) potatoes
1 large bunch of herbs of
   choice
2½ pints (1.4 litres) vegetable
   stock
¼ pint (150ml) goat's milk
   yogurt
Juice of ½ a lemon
Sea salt
Freshly ground black pepper

(Illustrated opposite.)

SCRUB AND dice the potatoes. Trim the herbs and chop finely, reserving a little for a garnish. Bring the stock to the boil, add the potatoes and herbs. Cover and simmer for 25 minutes, allow to cool and then liquidize.

Stir the yogurt and lemon juice into the soup. Season to taste. Chill thoroughly and serve garnished with the remaining herbs.

Note:
Choose mild green herbs such as parsley, coriander, chervil, dill, sorrel, watercress or mint — either individually or as a mixture. Lemon balm or verbena, or one of the more unusual mints, could be used for a more strongly flavoured soup.

Carrot and Orange Soup

3 oz (75g) butter
2 cloves garlic, crushed
1 medium onion, sliced
1 lb (450g) carrots, scrubbed
    and sliced
1½ pints (850ml) milk
Sea salt
Freshly ground black pepper
Zest of 2 oranges
½ pint (300ml) freshly
    squeezed orange juice
¼ pint (150ml) sherry
Vegetable stock, to taste
1 tablespoon freshly chopped
    coriander
¼ pint (150ml) whipped
    cream

MELT THE butter and lightly sauté the garlic and onion until soft. Add the carrots and toss in the butter. Stir in the milk and simmer until the carrots are tender. Season to taste.

Cool and then liquidize. Stir in the orange zest, juice and sherry. If the soup is too thick for your liking, stir in sufficient stock to thin it down. Stir together the coriander and cream, and beat in a little extra sherry.

Chill the soup and serve with a heaped teaspoon of the cream mixture floating on the surface of each bowl.

1 oz (25g) butter
1 large onion, chopped
1¾ pints (1 litre) water
8 fl oz (250ml) Dão red wine
7 oz (200g) red lentils
2 unsalted vegetable stock
   cubes
5 oz (140g) tomato purée
1 teaspoon raw cane sugar
4 bay leaves
Sea salt
Freshly ground black pepper
¼ pint (150ml) single cream
Freshly chopped parsley to
   garnish

Red Wine and Lentil Soup

HEAT THE butter in a large pan and sauté the onion until golden brown. Add the water, wine, lentils, stock cubes, tomato purée, sugar and bay leaves. Bring to the boil, cover and simmer until the lentils are cooked — about 40 minutes.

Remove the bay leaves. Blend the soup very briefly, season to taste, reheat and serve garnished with cream and parsley. Warm wholemeal garlic bread is good with this soup.

1 oz (25g) butter
3 red peppers, seeded and
 chopped
1 lb (450g) leeks, cleaned and
 sliced
Pinch powdered ginger, to
 taste
Pinch ground cumin, to taste
Pinch sweet paprika, to taste
1 oz (25g) fresh ginger, grated
Zest and juice of 1 orange
2 pints (1.1 litres) carrot stock
1 pint (600ml) buttermilk
Sea salt
Freshly ground black pepper

1½ cucumbers, chopped
1 lb (450g) fromage blanc
3 heaped tablespoons natural
 yogurt
Sea salt
Freshly ground black pepper
½ cucumber for garnish
Freshly chopped dill weed for
 garnish

Potage Crème de Piments Glacé au Gingembre

HEAT THE butter in a large pan and sauté the peppers and leeks until soft. Stir in the spices, orange zest and juice and the carrot stock. Bring to the boil and simmer for 30 minutes.

Cool the soup, liquidize and then refrigerate. When well chilled, stir in the buttermilk and season to taste. Return the soup to the fridge to chill before serving.

Note:
To make the carrot stock, cook 2 lb (900g) sliced carrots and 2 chopped onions in 2½ pints (1.4 litres) water with 1 crushed clove of garlic and 1 finely chopped shallot for 1 hour, then strain before use.

Chilled Cucumber Soup

PLACE THE first three ingredients in a blender or food processor and purée to a smooth soup. Pour into a bowl and season to taste. Chill well before serving garnished with finely diced cucumber and chopped dill weed.

Mangetout Soup

8 oz (225g) mangetout peas
2 oz (50g) butter
2 level tablespoons wholemeal
   flour
1½ pints (850ml) water
2 unsalted vegetable stock
   cubes
Sea salt
Freshly ground black pepper
Pinch raw cane sugar
   (optional)
¼ pint (150ml) single cream
Marigold petals for garnish

TOP AND TAIL the mangetout peas. Heat the butter in a large pan and sauté the mangetouts for about 5 minutes, then stir in the flour and cook briefly. Gradually pour in the water, add the stock cubes and bring to the boil. Simmer for 10 to 15 minutes until the peas are tender. ·

Purée the soup in a blender or processor, return it to the pan and heat through. Season to taste with salt, pepper and sugar if wished. Serve with a swirl of cream and a sprinkling of marigold petals in each bowl.

Red Pepper and Coconut Soup

4 oz (100g) desiccated coconut
2 pints (1.1 litres) hot
   skimmed milk
2 strips lemon rind
2 large red peppers, seeded
   and diced
Creamed coconut to taste
Sea salt
Freshly ground black pepper
Pinch raw cane sugar

SOAK THE coconut in the hot milk with the lemon strips for 30 minutes. Strain well and place the milk in a pan with the diced red pepper. Bring to the boil and simmer until the pepper is soft. Blend until smooth, then return the soup to the pan. Reheat, adding small pieces of creamed coconut until the soup is your chosen consistency and flavour. Season with salt, pepper and sugar.

In summer, serve this soup thin and chilled, in winter serve it thicker and hot.

Creamed Cashew Nut Soup

1 small onion
4 oz (100g) carrots
1 oz (25g) butter
3 oz (75g) cashew nuts
1 oz (25g) ground almonds
½ pint (300ml) milk
½ pint (300ml) water
2 teaspoons freshly chopped borage
Sea salt
Freshly ground black pepper
¼ pint (150ml) natural yogurt

FINELY CHOP the onion. Scrub and grate the carrots. Heat the butter in a pan and sauté the carrots and onion until soft. Grind the cashew nuts and add to the pan with the ground almonds. Cook for a few minutes, stirring.

Add the milk and water, bring to the boil and simmer for 10 to 15 minutes. Liquidize the soup, then return to the pan. Season to taste. Serve hot, with a blob of yogurt floating on the surface of each bowl.

Chilled Chick Pea and Lemon Soup

12 oz (340g) chick peas
1 lemon
½ pint (300ml) Greek yogurt
Sea salt
Freshly ground black pepper

SOAK THE chick peas for 8 hours or overnight. Drain and rinse them, then place in a large pan with the lemon, cut in half. Cover with fresh water, bring to the boil and simmer until the chick peas are tender.

Drain the cooked chick peas, reserving the cooking liquid but discarding the lemon. Purée the chick peas in a blender or food processor with enough cooking liquid to make a creamy soup the consistency of whipped cream. Stir in some yogurt to lighten the soup. Chill and serve garnished with a spoonful of yogurt in each bowl.

Avocado Terrine

3 avocados
Juice of ½ lemon
Juice of ½ lime
1 crushed clove garlic
Juice from 1 tablespoon
    crushed onion
12 fl oz (350ml) thick natural
    yogurt
12 fl oz (350ml) double cream
Sea salt
Freshly ground black pepper
West Indian hot pepper sauce
2 tablespoons Vinho Verde
    white wine
1 level teaspoon agar-agar

RESERVE one avocado. Halve and stone the others and scoop the flesh into a food processor or blender. Add the lemon and lime juice, garlic and onion juice, yogurt and cream. Blend to a purée, then season with salt, pepper and hot pepper sauce to taste.

Bring the white wine to the boil, add the agar-agar and dissolve as instructed on the packet. Then beat into the avocado purée. Spoon half the mixture into a loaf tin.

Halve, stone, peel and slice the remaining avocado and lay slices onto the purée. Top with the remaining purée and level the top. Refrigerate until set, then unmould and serve in slices on individual serving plates, garnished with cherry tomatoes and wild parsley. Offer melba toast to your guests when serving.

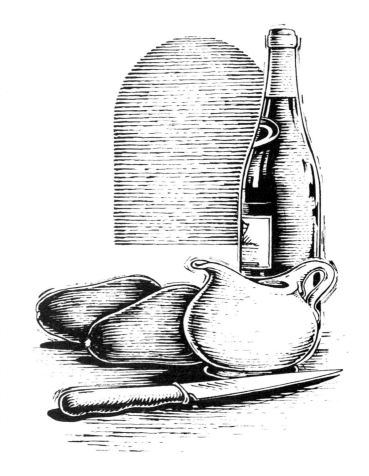

Choux Puffs with Avocado

16 choux pastry 'profiteroles'
2 large ripe avocados
1 small egg, separated
Squeeze of lemon juice
1 heaped tablespoon
    mayonnaise
Sea salt
Freshly ground black pepper
2 oz (50g) shelled pistachio
    nuts

(Illustrated opposite.)

Mᴀᴋᴇ ᴀ sʟɪᴛ in the sides of the choux pastry puffs, large enough to insert the filling through.

Halve and stone the avocados, then scoop the flesh into a bowl and mash well. Separate the egg and beat the yolk into the avocado pulp. Stir in the lemon juice and mayonnaise and season to taste. Whisk the egg white stiffly and fold this into the avocado mixture.

Use a teaspoon to insert filling into the profiteroles. Pile them onto a serving plate and sprinkle with chopped pistachio nuts. Serve at once.

Note:
Ready-made profiteroles can be purchased from a good patisserie, or can easily be made using a standard recipe and then frozen.

Individual Jalapeño Chilli Puffs

2 jalapeño chillis
3 oz (75g) grated mature
   Cheddar cheese
Sea salt
1 oz (25g) butter
¼ pint (150ml) soured cream
2 eggs, separated

SET THE oven to 400°F/200°C (Gas Mark 6).
   Finely chop the chillis and mix with the grated cheese and a little salt. Divide this mixture between 4 buttered ramekins.

Mix the soured cream with the egg yolks. Whisk the whites stiffly and fold them into the cream mixture. Spoon this carefully over the cheese. Place the ramekins in the oven for 10 to 15 minutes, until well-risen and golden. Serve at once.

Tomato Sorbet

1 lb (450g) ripe tomatoes
8 large tomatoes, for serving
Juice of ½ lemon
1 tablespoon tomato purée
1 sherry glass cream sherry
1 teaspoon vegetarian
   Worcestershire sauce
Sea salt
Freshly ground black pepper
2 egg whites

CHOP THE pound of tomatoes. Scoop the flesh from the large tomatoes, then place the shells upside down to drain. Place all the tomato flesh in a pan with the lemon juice and simmer, covered, until reduced and pulpy.

Sieve the cooked tomato flesh and mix with the tomato purée, sherry, Worcestershire sauce and seasoning. Freeze until slushy.

Blend the semi-frozen mixture until smooth. Beat the egg whites stiffly and fold into the tomato mixture. Freeze.

Remove the sorbet from the freezer 30 minutes before serving. Pile into the tomato shells and serve at once.

Leek, Almond and Tarragon Custards with Red Pepper Chutney

For the custard:
1 oz (25g) butter
1 lb (450g) thinly sliced whites of leek
1 tablespoon slivered, blanched almonds
1 tablespoon finely chopped tarragon
2 egg yolks and 1 egg, beaten
½ pint (300ml) double cream
Sea salt
Freshly ground black pepper
1 oz (25g) butter

For the chutney:
2 seeded and diced red peppers
1 finely chopped chilli
1 oz (25g) root ginger, chopped
2 tablespoons pounded coriander seeds
3 tablespoons raw cane sugar
Juice of ½ a lemon

HEAT THE butter in a pan and sauté the leeks very gently until meltingly soft. Pass through a sieve into a bowl and fold in the almonds and tarragon. Stir in the eggs and cream, and season to taste.

Spoon the mixture into four buttered ramekins, place in a bain marie and bake at 350°F/180°C (Gas Mark 4) until just set, taking care not to overcook.

While the custards are cooking, stew together all the ingredients for the chutney until soft and thickened. Place a spoonful of chutney onto each plate and unmould a custard alongside it. Serve at once.

33

Watercress Roulade
with Red Pepper Sauce

For the sauce:
½ oz (15g) butter
½ onion, finely chopped
2 fat cloves garlic, crushed
2 medium red peppers, seeded
   and diced
¼ pint (150ml) water
2 tablespoons Dão red wine
2 sprigs parsley, finely
   chopped
Sea salt
Cayenne pepper

For the roulade:
4 oz (100g) watercress
½ oz (15g) butter
2 eggs, separated
Sea salt
Freshly ground black pepper
1 oz (25g) toasted jumbo oats

(Illustrated opposite.)

FIRST, MAKE the sauce. Heat the butter in a pan and sauté the onion and garlic until translucent. Stir in the peppers and cook briefly. Then add the water, wine and parsley. Season with salt and cayenne and leave to simmer for 15 minutes until the peppers are cooked and the mixture has thickened somewhat. Purée the sauce in a processor or blender and set aside until ready to serve the roulade.

To prepare the roulade, bring a pan of salted water to the boil and plunge in the watercress. Simmer for 2 minutes then drain and squeeze out any excess moisture. Place the watercress in a food processor or blender and chop finely.

Add the butter and egg yolks to the machine and process again. Whisk the egg whites until stiff and fold in the watercress mixture. Season to taste.

Line a Swiss-roll tin with greaseproof paper and pour the mixture onto this. Bake at 400°F/200°C (Gas Mark 6) for 15 to 20 minutes, when the mixture should be firm to the touch. Sprinkle a fresh piece of greaseproof paper with the oats, then turn the watercress sponge out onto this.

While the roulade is baking, reheat the sauce so that it is ready to serve. Spread a little onto the roulade, then roll up in Swiss-roll fashion. Spoon a little more sauce onto 4 serving plates and slice the roulade so that a slice may be laid on each plate. Garnish with sprigs of fresh watercress and serve at once.

Individual Broccoli Soufflé Tartlets

4 oz (100g) rich shortcrust
    pastry
1 lb (450g) broccoli
1 oz (25g) butter
1 tablespoon unbleached
    white flour
¼ pint (150ml) milk
4 large eggs, separated
Sea salt
Freshly ground black pepper
Freshly grated nutmeg

LINE 4 INDIVIDUAL tartlet tins with the pastry and bake blind in a hot oven for 10 minutes.

Steam the broccoli until tender, then purée it in a food processor or blender.

Make a thick béchamel sauce with the butter, flour and milk, and fold the broccoli into this. Remove from the heat and beat in the egg yolks. Season well with salt, pepper and nutmeg.

Stiffly whisk the egg whites and fold into the broccoli mixture. Spoon this into the tartlet bases. Return the tartlet tins to the oven and cook at 400°F/200°C (Gas Mark 6) for 20 to 25 minutes, by which time they will be puffed up and golden brown.

Serve at once with a salad of French beans and shredded curly lettuce.

Note:
The bases can be made well in advance, as can the filling up to the point just before the eggs are added.

Fennel and Avocado Roulade

For the roulade:
1 oz (25g) butter
¾ oz (20g) flour
½ pint (300ml) warm milk
2 oz (50g) grated mature
    Cheddar cheese
2 eggs, separated
Sea salt
Freshly ground black pepper

For the filling:
1 small bulb fennel
1 oz (25g) butter
1 ripe avocado
Parmesan cheese

PREPARE A roux with the butter and flour, and gradually stir in the warm milk to make a smooth béchamel sauce. Add the grated cheese and allow to melt. Cool the sauce to blood heat, then beat in the egg yolks. Stiffly whisk the egg whites and fold into the cheese sauce. Season to taste.

Line a Swiss-roll tin with greaseproof paper and pour the mixture into this. Bake at 400°F/200°C (Gas Mark 6) for 15 minutes.

Meanwhile, finely chop the fennel and toss in melted butter over a low heat until just softened. Halve, stone and dice the avocado and stir this into the fennel. Remove from the heat.

When the roulade is cooked, remove from the oven and turn out onto a fresh piece of greaseproof paper that has been dusted with Parmesan cheese. Spread with filling and roll up. Serve at once.

SECOND PRIZE MENU

Caroline Stay

(Illustrated overleaf.)

FIRST COURSE
Spinach and Lemon Mousselines with Avocado
WINE: Vinho Verde

MAIN COURSE
Pasta and Mangetout in Butter Ginger Sauce with Cashews and Almonds
WINE: Dão Grão Vasco

SIDE DISH
Mushrooms Stuffed with Onion and Garlic Purée

SALAD
Palm Heart and Artichoke Salad

CHEESES
Two-year-old Gouda, Blue Stilton, Farmhouse Caerphilly
WINE: Château Doisy-Daëne 1979

PUDDING
Honeyed Greek Raspberries
WINE: Château Doisy-Daëne 1979

Spinach and Lemon Mousselines with Avocado

7 oz (200g) spinach
1½ tablespoons lemon juice
2 large eggs
7 fl oz (210ml) double cream
Sea salt
Freshly ground black pepper
1 oz (25g) butter
1 large avocado

For the dressing:
1 tablespoon lemon juice
2 tablespoons olive oil
1 teaspoon honey
Sea salt
Freshly ground black pepper

TRIM THE stalks from the spinach. You should end up with about 5 oz (150g). Wash it well, then place in a pan with just the water that clings to the leaves. Cover and cook until tender. Drain well and cool. When the spinach is cold, liquidize with the lemon juice until smooth. Add the eggs and blend again. Add the cream and seasoning and blend once more.

Lightly grease 4 ramekins, and pour in the spinach cream. Cover with circles of greased foil. Place in a bain marie and bake at 375°F/190°C (Gas Mark 5) for 40 minutes, or until set.

Meanwhile, slice the avocado thinly and heat all the dressing ingredients gently together. When the mousselines are cooked, run a sharp knife around the sides and turn out onto warmed serving plates. Garnish with slices of avocado and drizzle a little warmed dressing over each portion.

For the pasta:
4 oz (100g) strong plain flour
1 large egg
1 tablespoon vegetable oil
1 tablespoon water
½ teaspoon sea salt

For the sauce:
4 fl oz (120ml) orange juice
¼ pint (150ml) white wine
  vinegar
2-inch (5cm) piece root ginger,
  peeled and chopped
24 cardamom pods, bruised
4 teaspoons coriander seeds
1 strip orange peel
6-8 oz (150-225g) butter
4 pieces preserved ginger in
  syrup
1 orange

To assemble the dish:
8 oz (225g) mangetout peas
1 oz (25g) butter
3 oz (75g) cashew nuts
3 oz (75g) blanched almonds
Sea salt
Freshly ground black pepper

Pasta and Mangetout in Butter Ginger Sauce with Cashews and Almonds

FIRST, MAKE the pasta by processing all the ingredients together until the dough is smooth and elastic. Wrap in clingfilm and leave to rest.

Place the orange juice, vinegar, root ginger, cardamom pods, coriander and the strip of orange peel in a pan and reduce slowly until there are only about 4 tablespoons left. Strain and set aside. Cut the butter into small pieces and refrigerate. Cut the preserved ginger into julienne strips. Finely grate the orange rind and thinly slice the flesh.

Roll out the pasta dough very thinly and cut into strips about the same size and shape as the mangetout pods. Cook the pasta in boiling salted water. Top and tail the mangetouts and stir-fry them in a little butter.

Reheat the sauce to boiling point and whisk in the pieces of butter bit by bit, off the heat. Drain the pasta and mix with the mangetout. Add the preserved ginger and the grated orange rind to the sauce. Dry roast the nuts briefly in salt and pepper.

Arrange the pasta and mangetout on a warm serving dish, pour over the sauce and sprinkle with nuts. Garnish with slices of orange and serve at once.

Mushrooms Stuffed with Onion and Garlic Purée

1 lb (450g) Spanish onions
1 head of garlic
½ oz (15g) butter
Sea salt
Freshly ground black pepper
1½ oz (45g) Parmesan cheese
12 medium sized mushrooms

PEEL AND dice the onions roughly. Peel the garlic. Heat the butter in a pan and cook the onion and garlic together very gently, until meltingly tender. Liquidize or process with a little salt and lots of black pepper. Stir in the Parmesan cheese.

Clean the mushrooms and remove their stalks. Use a teaspoon to fill the mushrooms with the onion and garlic mixture. Place, stuffing side up, in a greased ovenproof dish and cover with foil. Bake at 375°F/190°C (Gas Mark 5) for 30 minutes, then serve at once.

Palm Heart and Artichoke Salad

2 globe artichokes
1 tablespoon lemon juice
½ tin palm hearts
4 tablespoons olive oil
   flavoured with basil
1 tablespoon white wine
   vinegar
Sea salt
Freshly ground black pepper

CUT THE stalks off the artichokes and rub the bases with lemon juice. Cook in acidulated boiling water for 20 to 25 minutes until the leaves pull away easily from the head. Drain well, upside down. Remove all the leaves and scrape away the hairy choke. Reserve the larger leaves, discarding the rest along with the choke. Slice the bases into julienne strips.

Slice the palm hearts into julienne strips. Mix together the oil, vinegar and seasoning in a screw top jar. Place the artichoke and palm hearts in a salad bowl and dress with a little vinaigrette. Arrange the reserved leaves around the edge in a water lily pattern. Serve at once.

Honeyed Greek Raspberries

8 oz (225g) raspberries
4 teaspoons clear honey,
   preferably Greek
½ pint (300ml) Greek 'Total'
   yogurt
4 heaped teaspoons raw cane
   sugar
Mint leaves, to garnish

RESERVE 4 raspberries for a garnish, and divide the rest between 4 bowls. Spoon the honey over them. Top with the yogurt, then sprinkle on the sugar. Decorate with reserved raspberries and fresh mint leaves. Chill for 2 hours before serving.

MAIN COURSES

Buckwheat Crêpes Gâteau

For the crêpes:
4 oz (100g) buckwheat flour
½ pint (300ml) milk
3 eggs, beaten
½ teaspoon sea salt
2 tablespoons vegetable oil,
    plus extra for frying

For the filling:
1½ lb (650g) fresh spinach
3 tablespoons butter
1 tablespoon flour
½ pint (300ml) milk
Sea salt
Freshly ground black pepper
Freshly grated nutmeg

For the sauce:
8 oz (225g) button mushrooms
3 tablespoons butter
1 tablespoon flour
¼-½ pint (150-300ml) milk
Sea salt
Freshly ground black pepper

PLACE THE flour in a bowl and beat in half the milk, followed by the eggs, salt and 2 tablespoons of oil. Leave to stand for 2 hours, then add the rest of the milk. Make 10 to 12 crêpes of equal size — about 8 or 9 inches (20-23cm) in diameter. Set aside.

Remove any coarse stems from the spinach and wash well. Place in a large pan with just the water that clings to the leaves. Cover tightly and cook for 5 minutes. Remove from the heat, rinse in cold water and drain well. Chop the spinach finely.

Make a white sauce with the butter, flour and milk. Stir in the spinach. The mixture should have the consistency of thick cream. Season with salt, pepper and nutmeg.

Grease the bottom of a round ovenproof dish and place the thickest crêpe you have made in the bottom. Spread with a little filling to within ½ inch (1cm) of the edge. Repeat until all the crêpes and filling are used, with the top crêpe uncovered.

Quarter the mushrooms and sauté in the butter. Make a roux with the flour, then add enough milk to make a thick sauce. Season to taste, then spread the sauce over the gâteau as if icing a cake.

Bake in a preheated oven at 375°F/190°C (Gas Mark 5) for 30 minutes. Serve, sliced like a cake, with yellow courgettes lightly poached in milk as a vegetable side dish.

Gruyère Gougère with Leek, Mushroom and Caper Cream Sauce

For the gougère:
1 pint (600ml) milk
4 oz (100g) butter
6 oz (150g) unbleached white
  flour
8 eggs, beaten
8 oz (225g) grated Gruyère
  cheese
Sea salt
Freshly ground black pepper
Extra butter for greasing tin

For the sauce:
2 lb (900g) leeks
3 oz (75g) butter
12 oz (350g) field mushrooms
4 tablespoons drained capers
Sea salt
Freshly ground black pepper
Garlic salt
Chopped fresh oregano
8 fl oz (250ml) single cream

T O MAKE the gougère, bring the milk and butter to the boil in a large pan, stirring well to mix the melted butter. Sift the flour in gradually, beating well as you do so. When the mixture is smooth, beat in the eggs one at a time. Beat the mixture energetically, so that it becomes glossy and smooth. Fold in 3 oz (75g) of the cheese.

Spoon or pipe the mixture into a well-greased pavlova tin. Sprinkle with the remaining cheese and place in a preheated oven at 375°F/190°C (Gas Mark 5) for 45 minutes, until puffed and golden-brown.

Meanwhile, clean the leeks well and slice them thinly. Melt the butter in a pan and sauté the leeks until soft. Add the mushrooms to the pan and cook gently. Stir in the capers, seasoning and herbs. Just before the gougère is cooked, stir the cream into the vegetables and warm through.

Remove the gougère from the oven, open the tin and lift the ring out onto a warm plate, glossy cheese side uppermost. Fill the centre with the sauce and decorate the outside with chicory and baby tomatoes. Serve at once.

1 medium aubergine
Sea salt
3 fl oz (90ml) olive oil
3 medium tomatoes, skinned
  and chopped
2 tablespoons tomato purée
1 clove garlic, crushed
1 teaspoon chopped fresh basil
1 teaspoon chopped fresh
  marjoram
Freshly ground black pepper
½ onion, chopped
2 sticks celery, chopped
2 fl oz (60ml) water
4 oz (100g) chopped walnuts
1 oz (25g) wholemeal
  breadcrumbs
8 oz (225g) courgettes, sliced
1 tablespoon chopped chives
1 tablespoon single cream
8 oz (225g) puff pastry
1 egg, beaten, to glaze

Légumes et Noisettes en Croûte

DICE THE aubergine and sprinkle with salt. Leave for 30 minutes to release its bitter juices, then rinse and dry. Heat one-third of the oil in a pan and sauté the aubergine briefly. Then add the tomatoes, tomato purée, garlic, herbs and seasoning. Cook gently until the aubergine is tender.

Heat half of the remaining oil in a pan. Sauté the onion and celery until soft, then add water and stir in the chopped nuts and breadcrumbs. Cook briefly, season to taste, then set aside.

Heat the remaining oil in a pan. Sauté the sliced courgettes until just tender, then blend briefly in a liquidizer or food processor. Stir in the chives and cream, and season to taste.

Roll out the pastry and cut two 10-inch (30cm) circles. Lay one on a greased baking tin or in a pie dish. Place layers of filling in the centre — first the nut filling, then the aubergine, and last the courgettes. Cover with the second circle of pastry and brush the edges with egg before pinching to seal them. Brush the top of the pastry with more egg wash. Decorate the pie with trimmings if wished.

Place in a preheated oven at 450°F/230°C (Gas Mark 8) for 15 minutes, then lower the temperature to 400°F/200°C (Gas Mark 6) and cook for a further 30 minutes. Serve cut into wedges.

Individual Sweet Potato Soufflés

6 oz (150g) sweet potatoes, peeled

½ pint (300ml) Cyprus sheep's yogurt

3 eggs, separated

A small bunch of chopped spring onions

2 oz (50g) grated Pecorino cheese

Sea salt

Freshly ground black pepper

Pinch of cream of tartar

1 oz (25g) butter

STEAM THE sweet potatoes until tender, then mash well. Blend in the yogurt, egg yolks, spring onions, cheese and seasoning. Whisk the egg whites until stiff, with a pinch of cream of tartar. Fold into the potato mixture.

Grease 4 ramekins and divide the mixture between them. Bake for 20 minutes at 350°F/180°C (Gas Mark 4), when the soufflés will be risen and golden. Serve at once with a creamy herb and mushroom sauce.

Souffléed Potato Pancakes with Buttered Asparagus

Per person:

4 oz (100g) boiled, sieved Maris
   Piper potatoes
2 eggs, separated
Sea salt
Freshly ground black pepper
4 oz (100g) butter
4 oz (100g) steamed asparagus
   tips

BEAT TOGETHER the sieved potato and the egg yolks. Season with salt and pepper. Stiffly whisk the egg whites and fold them into the mixture.

Reserving a quarter of the butter for the pancake, heat the rest gently in a pan and toss the asparagus in this. Keep warm, shaking the pan occasionally, while you make the pancake.

Heat the remaining butter in a 6-inch (15cm) cast iron pan and tip in the pancake mixture. Cook on one side until golden, then turn and immediately spoon on the asparagus. Fold and serve as soon as the pancake is puffed and risen.

Spinach Rounds

8 oz (225g) fresh spinach
½ onion, finely chopped
1 egg, beaten
Fresh wholemeal
    breadcrumbs, to bind and
    coat
Sea salt
Freshly ground black pepper
Vegetable oil, for frying

WASH THE spinach well and strip off any coarse stems or damaged leaves. Place in a pan with just the water that clings to the leaves, cover and simmer until cooked. Chop very finely.

Place the spinach in a bowl and stir in the chopped onion. Beat in the egg, and then add sufficient breadcrumbs to make a stiff mixture. Season well.

Shape the mixture into 4 round, flattish cakes of equal size. Coat both sides in breadcrumbs. Heat the oil in a pan and sauté the cakes on both sides until golden and sizzling. Serve with a creamy vegetable dish such as Eliza Acton's Creamed Cucumbers.

Pastry Tarts with Three Fillings and Three Sauces

20 individual wholemeal
   pastry tart shells

*For the mushroom and
walnut filling:*
1 oz (25g) butter
8 oz (225g) mushrooms
2 oz (50g) walnuts
Sea salt
Freshly ground black pepper
Mushroom ketchup

*For the broad bean, basil and
pine kernel filling:*
8 oz (225g) broad beans
1 tablespoon fresh basil leaves
1 oz (25g) butter
1 oz (25g) pine kernels
1 tablespoon olive oil

*For the courgette, pimento
and onion filling:*
2 fl oz (60ml) olive oil
8 oz (225g) courgettes, thinly
   sliced
1 small onion, finely chopped
1 clove garlic, crushed
½ yellow pepper, seeded and
   sliced

(Illustrated opposite.)

PREPARE THE pastry shells, but do not bake until the fillings and sauces have been made. First, make the fillings. Heat the butter in a pan and sauté the mushrooms lightly, then place in a blender with the walnuts and purée until fairly smooth. Season with salt, pepper and mushroom ketchup. Keep warm.

Remove the broad beans from their pods and cook until tender. Purée half of them with the basil. Skin the remaining beans and stir in, along with the butter. Sauté the pine kernels in olive oil. Keep warm.

Heat half the olive oil in a pan and sauté the courgettes, onion and garlic, then purée and keep warm. Sauté the yellow pepper in the remaining oil and keep warm.

(Continued overleaf.)

*For the redcurrant and
wine sauce:*
8 oz (225g) redcurrant jelly
8 fl oz (250ml) Dão red wine
Pinch cayenne pepper
Shoyu sauce
1 dessertspoon cornflour
A little water

*For the marsala, cream and
nutmeg sauce:*
8 fl oz (250ml) double cream
3 fl oz (90ml) marsala
Freshly grated nutmeg
Sea salt
Freshly ground black pepper

*For the lemon and
white wine sauce:*
½ pint (300ml) Vinho Verde
    white wine
1 teaspoon aniseed cloves
Juice and finely grated rind of
    3 lemons
Pinch raw cane sugar
Shoyu sauce
Natural yellow food colour
    (optional)
2 tablespoons cornflour
A little water

NEXT, MAKE the sauces. Heat together in a pan the redcurrant jelly and the red wine. Season with cayenne and add a splash of shoyu. Thicken with a slurry of cornflour and water and simmer to cook the flour. Keep warm.

Boil the cream and marsala together in another pan until thickened. Season with salt, pepper and plenty of nutmeg. Keep warm.

Bring the white wine to the boil with the aniseeds. Strain and stir in the lemon rind and juice. Season with a little sugar, to taste, and a splash of shoyu. Add a drop of natural yellow food colouring if wished. Return to the pan and thicken with a slurry of cornflour. Keep warm.

Bake the tarts just before serving, at 400°F/200°C (Gas Mark 6) until crisp and golden. Fill some with the first filling. Fill some with the second, sprinkling the pine kernels on the top. Fill the rest with the third, putting courgette purée in first, then laying slices of pepper over the top. The fillings should all be warm, but not hot.

Serve one of each tartlet to each person, putting the rest on a large dish in the centre of the table, so that your guests can help themselves to more of those they like best.

Serve the sauces, warm to hot, in jugs. Let your guests help themselves.

Savoury Rye Pancakes

For the batter:
1 large egg
2 oz (50g) strong unbleached white flour
2 oz (50g) rye flour
½ pint (300ml) mixture of milk and water
Vegetable oil, for frying

For the spinach and walnut stuffing:
8 oz (225g) fresh spinach
2 oz (50g) coarsely chopped walnuts
Sea salt
Freshly ground black pepper
Freshly grated nutmeg

For the mushrooms and aubergine stuffing:
1 medium aubergine
4 oz (100g) button mushrooms
1 oz (25g) butter
1 fl oz (30ml) olive oil
Sea salt
Freshly ground black pepper

TO MAKE the batter, simply place all the ingredients, except the oil for frying, in a food processor or liquidizer and blend briefly until smooth. Chill before use. Lightly brush a frying pan with oil and leave on a very low heat for 15 to 20 minutes to 'prove' before use. Turn up the heat, add a little more oil and heat it through, then pour in just enough batter to make a pancake about 7 or 8 inches (18 or 20cm) across. Cook on both sides, then reserve on kitchen paper. Make 7 more pancakes of a similar size and set aside while you make the fillings.

Wash the spinach and remove any coarse stems or damaged leaves. Place in a pan, cover tightly, and cook for 3 to 5 minutes. Drain well, chop roughly, stir in the walnuts and season to taste. Set aside.

Wash the aubergine and dice it evenly. Wash the mushrooms and halve or quarter if large. Heat the oil and butter and cook the aubergines until softened, then add the mushrooms and cook briefly. Season to taste.

Divide each filling between 4 pancakes and roll up. Place them in an ovenproof dish and reheat under a hot grill until warmed through and starting to brown on top. Serve at once.

For the pastry:
12 oz (350g) wholemeal flour
3 teaspoons baking powder
Sea salt
3 fl oz (90ml) sunflower oil
Water to mix

For the filling:
6 cloves garlic, finely chopped
1 small red chilli, finely
   chopped
3 tablespoons chopped fresh
   parsley
½ teaspoon crushed coriander
   seeds
3 tablespoons olive oil
1 glass Vinho Verde white
   wine
1 lb (450g) onions
Sea salt
Freshly ground black pepper
Beaten egg, to glaze

(Illustrated opposite.)

Onion Pasties

SIFT THE flour, baking powder and salt into a bowl, adding back any bran left in the sieve. Into this, beat the oil, and then add water little-by-little until a smooth pastry is formed. Roll into a ball and set aside, covered, to relax.

In a small pan, place the garlic, chilli, 1 tablespoon of the parsley, the coriander seeds, and 1 tablespoon of the oil. Sauté until sizzling and nut-brown. Add the wine and simmer for a few minutes.

Slice the onion finely and place in a bowl with the remaining parsley and oil, then tip in the contents of the pan. Season to taste, then set aside.

Roll the pastry out very thinly and cut into 6 equal squares. Divide these to give 12 triangles. With the long edge facing away from you, wet the other two edges. Place one-twelfth of the filling in the centre of each triangle. Now fold the long edge towards you and twist the end pieces to seal. Pull the ends round and join them together to make a shape like an oversized tortellini.

Place the pasties on a greased baking tray, brush with beaten egg and bake in a hot oven at 425°F/220°C (Gas Mark 7) for 10 minutes. Serve at once with a garnish of watercress and hand round Tomato Sauce (page 56).

1 clove garlic, crushed
1 small onion, finely chopped
1 tablespoon chopped fresh
   oregano
1 tablespoon chopped fresh
   parsley
2 tablespoons sunflower oil
1 wineglass madeira
1 lb (450g) tomatoes, skinned,
   seeded and chopped
Sea salt
Freshly ground black pepper

Tomato Sauce

FRY THE garlic, onion, oregano and parsley gently in the oil until soft. Pour in the madeira, then stir in the tomatoes. Simmer until the tomatoes have completely disintegrated, then sieve or liquidize, season to taste, and serve.

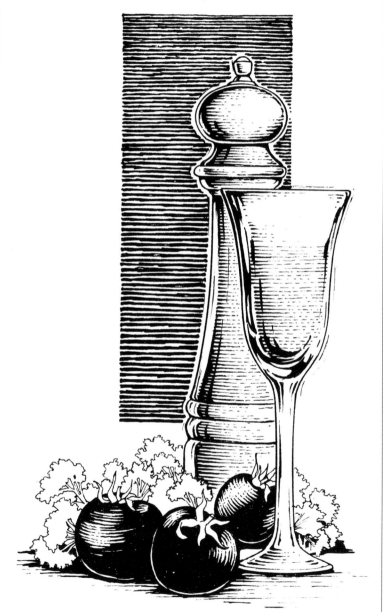

Poached Spinach Sausages

1½ lb (650g) fresh spinach
4 oz (100g) unskinned roasted
   almonds, finely ground
1 egg white
2 egg yolks
4 oz (100g) pine nuts
Sea salt
Freshly ground black pepper
Freshly grated nutmeg
4 tablespoons chilled double
   cream

WASH THE spinach well, removing any coarse stems or damaged leaves. Place in a pan, cover and cook until just tender. Drain well, chop and return to the pan to dry out completely. Place in a food processor and purée until smooth. Stir in enough ground almonds to make a stiff, but not dry, mixture. With the motor running, add the egg white and yolks, and pine nuts to the mixture. Season and place in the freezer for 20 minutes.

Return the chilled mixture to the machine and process again. With the motor running, gradually pour in the chilled cream. Do not allow the purée to become too runny.

Test the mixture for seasoning and texture by poaching a spoonful in fast-simmering salted water until set.

Take 4 large squares of clingfilm and divide the mixture amongst them, forming into sausages about 7 inches (18cm) long. Make sure there are no air pockets before twisting the ends to seal the packets, and tying with string. Poach the sausages in simmering water for 15 minutes before unwrapping and serving.

Serve with a Tomato Sauce (such as that on page 56) and garnish with flaked almonds that have been sautéed in butter.

2½ oz (65g) strong plain
   wholemeal flour

Sea salt

Freshly ground black pepper

2 oz (50g) butter, cut into small
   pieces

¼ pint (150ml) cold water

2 eggs, beaten

A few strands saffron, soaked
   overnight in 1 tablespoon
   water

1½ oz (35g) grated Gruyère
   cheese

(Illustrated opposite.)

Saffron Gougère

SIFT THE flour and seasoning onto a large sheet of grease-proof paper. Place the butter and water in a pan and bring to the boil. As soon as it is boiling, tip in the seasoned flour all at once and beat well with a wooden spoon to make a smooth mixture that leaves the sides of the pan.

Remove the pan from the heat and leave to cool for 5 minutes. Then gradually beat in the eggs, reserving about 1 tablespoonful for glazing. Beat in the saffron and 1 tablespoonful of cheese. The mixture should be thick, smooth and glossy.

Rinse a baking tray in cold water, then spoon dessertspoonfuls of the mixture into a ring on the tray, about 7 inches (18cm) in diameter. Brush well with the reserved egg, and sprinkle with the cheese. Heat the oven to 425°F/220°C (Gas Mark 7) and put the baking sheet in near the top of the oven. After 20 minutes, reduce the heat to 375°F/190°C (Gas Mark 5) and bake for a further 10 minutes. Serve hot and puffy from the oven with Sorrel Sauce (page 60).

Sorrel Sauce

2 tablespoons vegetable oil
1 small onion, finely chopped
1 medium potato, peeled and
　diced
1 clove garlic, crushed
½ pint (300ml) vegetable stock
Juice of ½ a lemon
6 to 8 sorrel leaves, washed
　and shredded
Sea salt
Freshly ground black pepper
2 tablespoons soured cream

HEAT THE oil in a pan and sauté the onion, potato and garlic for 5 minutes, until soft but not browned. Place in a food processor or blender with the stock and lemon juice and purée briefly. Add the sorrel to the mixture and purée again until smooth. Season to taste.

Return the mixture to the pan and boil for 2 minutes. Stir in the cream just before serving.

Fresh Lasagne, Layered with Asparagus, Tomatoes and Mozzarella

Lasagne, made with 12 oz (350g) plain flour and 3 eggs
2 medium onions, roughly chopped
2 cloves garlic, crushed
2 tablespoons olive oil
1 lb (450g) tomatoes, skinned and chopped
1 tablespoon chopped fresh tarragon
Sea salt
Freshly ground black pepper
1 lb (450g) fresh asparagus, trimmed
8 oz (225g) large white mushrooms, sliced
2 oz (50g) butter
8 oz (225g) thinly sliced Mozzarella
1 pint (600ml) thick béchamel sauce

MAKE THE lasagne in the usual way, wrap in clingfilm and let rest in the fridge for 30 minutes. Then roll into strips and dry them for 10 to 15 minutes.

Sauté the onions and garlic in the olive oil for a few minutes, then add the tomatoes and cook until the sauce is rich and thick. Stir in the herbs and season to taste.

Steam the asparagus for 8 minutes. Cut into 1-inch (2.5cm) lengths. Sauté the mushrooms in the butter for almost 5 minutes, then add the asparagus to the pan for the last 30 seconds of cooking and stir well.

Cook the sheets of lasagne in boiling salted water in a large roasting tin on top of the cooker for 6 minutes. Drain and cool.

Butter a lasagne dish and build up the layers as follows: first, the asparagus and mushrooms mixture; then a layer of lasagne; then thinly sliced Mozzarella and another layer of lasagne; then tomato sauce and another layer of lasagne; and last, the béchamel sauce.

Bake the dish for 45 minutes at 375°F/190°C (Gas Mark 5). Serve with crispy fried cauliflower sprigs and freshly grated Parmesan cheese.

8 oz (225g) fresh asparagus,
  trimmed
8 oz (225g) shelled garden peas
4 tablespoons double cream
2 egg yolks
Sea salt
Freshly ground black pepper
1 oz (25g) butter

Petites Timbales Rayées

COOK THE asparagus and the peas separately, until tender. Place the asparagus in a food processor or liquidizer with 2 tablespoons of cream and 1 egg yolk. Purée until smooth, remove to a bowl and season to taste.

Clean the processor or blender and repeat this procedure with the cooked peas.

Lightly butter four 4-inch (10cm) ramekins. Spoon the purées into the ramekins in layers — two layers of each purée to each ramekin. Place the ramekins in a bain marie and poach in the oven at 375°F/190°C (Gas Mark 5) until lightly set.

When turned out onto serving plates the timbales will be in stripes of gently differing greens. Serve with a sauce *beurre blanc*, made with finely chopped shallots, a reduction of white wine vinegar and white wine, and fresh unsalted butter. Spoon just a little onto each plate alongside the timbale and serve at once.

Tagliatelle with Brie Sauce

1 lb (450g) home-made
   tagliatelle
8 oz (225g) broccoli florets
¼ pint (150ml) single cream
4 oz (100g) de-rinded Brie,
   diced
2 egg yolks
Sea salt
Freshly ground black pepper

BRING A large pan of salted water to the boil and cook the pasta and broccoli until both are just 'al dente'. While they are cooking, heat together the cream and cheese. As soon as the cheese has melted, remove the sauce from the heat and beat in the egg yolks to thicken the sauce. Season to taste. Serve the pasta and broccoli on a warmed serving dish with the sauce poured over the top.

Note:
Stilton would be a delicious alternative to Brie in this recipe.

12 oz (350g) silver beet (Swiss chard)
1 small bunch spring onions
3 oz (75g) butter
2 eggs, beaten
3 tablespoons double cream
1 oz (25g) Parmesan cheese
Sea salt
Freshly ground black pepper
1 8-inch (20cm) pastry case, baked blind
1 oz (25g) grated mature Cheddar cheese

Silver Beet (Swiss Chard) Flan

DROP THE silver beet leaves into a pan of rapidly boiling salted water and cook until tender. Rinse under cold running water then drain and squeeze out all excess water. Chop finely.

Chop the spring onions and fry in about two-thirds of the butter. Add the silver beet and cook until all the moisture has evaporated. Allow to cool.

Beat together the eggs, cream, Parmesan and seasoning. Stir in the beet and onion mixture. Pour into the pastry case and top with Cheddar cheese and dots of the remaining butter. Bake at 375°F/190°C (Gas Mark 5) for 25 to 35 minutes. Best served hot and puffed up, straight from the oven, but it tastes very good cold, too.

THIRD PRIZE MENU

Dominique Plumanns

(Illustrated overleaf.)

FIRST COURSE
Souffléed Aubergines with Souffléed Courgettes
WINE: Gazela Vinho Verde

MAIN COURSE
Field Mushrooms in a Red Wine Sabayon Sauce with Coriander, in a Pastry Bowl
WINE: Dão Grão Vasco

SIDE DISH
Three Green Beans Sautéed with Cumin

SALAD
Green Salad with Pine and Pistachio Nuts

CHEESES
Munster d'Alsace, Farmhouse Cheshire, Bleu de Bresse
WINE: Gewürztraminer d'Alsace 1981

PUDDING
Mango Sorbet with Strawberries
WINE: Gewürztraminer d'Alsace 1981

Souffléed Aubergines with Souffléed Courgettes

For the aubergines:
2 aubergines
1 small onion
2 teaspoons dry French
  vermouth
1 tablespoon olive oil
Sea salt
Freshly ground black pepper
Tomato purée
7 oz (200g) fromage blanc
2 egg yolks
2 egg whites

For the courgettes:
5 courgettes
2 tablespoons dry French
  vermouth
1 tablespoon olive oil
1 large clove garlic, bruised
2 sprigs thyme
Sea salt
Freshly ground black pepper
7 oz (200g) fromage blanc
2 egg yolks
2 egg whites

HEAT THE oven to 400°F/200°C (Gas Mark 6) and bake the aubergines for about 20 minutes, or until soft but still slightly springy. Allow to cool. Cut the cooled aubergines in half lengthways and carefully scoop out the flesh, leaving a thin shell. Chop the flesh and place in a blender or processor with the finely chopped onion and the vermouth. Blend until smooth.

In a non-stick pan, heat the olive oil, add the aubergine purée, salt, pepper and a squeeze of tomato purée. Cook until all moisture has evaporated, stirring frequently to stop the mixture burning. Cool. In a bowl, mix the fromage blanc and egg yolks until smooth. Add the aubergine mixture and sieve to make a smooth paste. In another bowl, beat the egg whites with a pinch of salt until stiff. Gradually fold in the vegetable purée, mixing carefully from the centre in one direction while turning the bowl in the other.

Cut four of the courgettes in half lengthways. Scoop out the flesh, leaving a thin shell. Chop the flesh. Peel and chop the fifth courgette. Place in a blender or processor with the vermouth and blend until smooth.

In a non-stick pan, heat the olive oil and sauté the garlic and thyme for 1 minute then add the courgette mixture and seasoning. Cook until all the moisture has evaporated, stirring to avoid the mixture burning. Cool, then proceed in the same way as for the aubergine soufflé mixture.

Fill the aubergine shells with the aubergine mixture, and the courgette shells with the courgette mixture. Place them in ovenproof dishes and bake at 400°F/200°C (Gas Mark 6) — the courgettes will take 20 to 25 minutes, the aubergines 20 to 30 minutes, depending on size.

Serve half an aubergine and two courgette halves per person, and decorate with courgette or nasturtium flowers.

Field Mushrooms in a Red Wine Sabayon Sauce with Coriander, in a Pastry Bowl

For the pastry:
8 oz (250g) flour
1 egg yolk
Sea salt
1 teaspoon cold water
4 oz (125g) butter

For the mushrooms:
1½-2 lb (650-900g) small field mushrooms
1 oz (25g) butter
1 tablespoon lemon juice
7 fl oz (200ml) Dão Grão Vasco red wine
2 fl oz (60ml) vegetable stock
Sea salt
Freshly ground black pepper
3 tablespoons chopped fresh coriander
2 egg yolks
6 tablespoons water
4 sprigs coriander, for garnish

MAKE THE pastry first. Sieve the flour into a bowl, make a well in the flour and add the egg yolk, salt and water. Mix a little. Add the chopped butter and mix with a spatula, then work in with the fingers and form into a ball. On a floured surface, work the pastry with your palms a couple of times. The mixture should be elastic. Cover and chill for 30 minutes, then use to line 4 individual ovenproof bowls. Bake blind at 400°F/200°C (Gas Mark 6) until cooked. Remove from the bowls and keep the pastry bowls just warm.

Wash and trim the mushrooms. Melt the butter in a non-stick pan and sauté the mushrooms for 30 seconds, then add the lemon juice and cook for another 30 seconds. Add the wine and stock, cover and cook for a few minutes. Remove the cooked mushrooms with a slotted spoon and keep warm.

Bring up the heat under the liquid and reduce by half before seasoning and adding the chopped coriander. Meanwhile beat together the egg yolks and water until foamy. Remove the pan of reduced liquid from the heat and whisk in the beaten egg mixture to make a light sabayon sauce.

Place the mushrooms in the pastry bowls, pour on a little sabayon sauce, decorate with coriander sprigs and serve at once.

Three Green Beans Sautéed with Cumin

8 oz (250g) shelled broad
 beans
8 oz (250g) French beans
8 oz (250g) mangetout
2 tablespoons mustard oil
1 tablespoon olive oil
¼ teaspoon asafoetida powder
1 teaspoon cumin seeds
1 clove garlic, slightly crushed
1 or 2 sprigs fresh thyme
1 bay leaf
Sea salt
Freshly ground black pepper

SKIN THE broad beans (or do so after blanching if necessary). Top and tail the French beans and mangetout. Wash and drain. Bring to the boil about 2 inches (5cm) salted water. Plunge in the broad beans to blanch, then remove them and rinse in cold water to refresh. Repeat this process with the French beans, cooking them until just tender but still crisp before refreshing. Reserve the cooking liquid.

In a heavy cast iron pan, heat the mustard and olive oils. Stir in the asafoetida powder then, after a second or two, the cumin seeds. As soon as they start to pop, add the garlic, thyme and bay leaf. Cook for a few more seconds, then stir in the French beans. Cook for 2 minutes, then add the mangetout. Cook for a further 2 minutes, then add the broad beans. Continue to cook, stirring, for 2 more minutes, then add 2 or 3 tablespoons of the bean cooking liquid. Cover and cook until everything is tender, adding more liquid as necessary. Remove the garlic, thyme and bay leaf before serving.

Green Salad with Pine and Pistachio Nuts

Lettuce leaves (of various types,
    as available)
Chicory (both red and white,
    if available)
2 tablespoons wine vinegar
3 tablespoons olive oil
Sea salt
Freshly ground black pepper
Finely chopped marjoram
1 ripe avocado
2-4 inch (3-10cm) piece
    cucumber, halved and sliced
1 oz (25g) shelled pistachio
    nuts
1 oz (25g) pine kernels

WASH THE salad leaves and drain well. In a small bowl, beat together the vinegar, oil, seasoning and marjoram to make a vinaigrette dressing. Peel, stone and slice the avocado and coat with a little dressing. In a salad bowl, toss the lettuce, chicory, cucumber and most of the nuts in the rest of the dressing. Place some of this on 4 serving plates, garnish with slices of avocado and sprinkle with the rest of the nuts.

Mango Sorbet
with Strawberries

2 medium sized mangoes
Juice of 1 lime
2½ oz (65g) sugar
4½ fl oz (125ml) water
7 fl oz (200ml) double cream
1-2 teaspoons sugar
2 teaspoons Kirsch
8 oz (250g) strawberries

HALVE, STONE and peel the mangoes, and chop the flesh. Place in a blender with the lime juice and blend until smooth.

Make a sugar syrup from the first batch of sugar and the water. Beat into the mango purée. Freeze until set.

Beat the cream until stiff, fold in a little sugar to taste and stir in the Kirsch. Freeze.

Chill 4 plates in the freezer. Thinly slice the strawberries. To serve, place a scoop of frozen cream in the centre of each plate, surround with 3 scoops of mango sorbet and decorate with slices of fresh strawberries.

SIDE DISHES

The Chef's Special Crunchy Rice

Short grain organic brown rice
Roughly chopped cashew nuts
Defrosted frozen sweetcorn
  kernels
Unrefined sesame oil, for
  frying
Sunflower seeds
Pumpkin seeds
Courgettes, coarsely grated
Shoyu sauce, to taste
Tahini, to taste

COOK YOUR required quantity of rice by your usual method. While it is cooking, prepare the other ingredients.

Lightly sauté the cashew nuts and sweetcorn kernels in a little sesame oil. Dry roast the seeds in a heavy cast iron pan until lightly toasted.

When the rice is cooked, stir in the sweetcorn and nuts, the seeds, and the courgettes. Flavour to your taste with shoyu and tahini, and serve at once.

This dish is always 'the chef's special' because the quantities of each ingredient will be to your own taste. However you choose, your rice will be full of complementary textures and pleasing contrasts of colour, as well as balanced protein.

For the skewers:
2 courgettes
16 button mushrooms
16 small round onions
16 cherry tomatoes

For the satay sauce:
1 tablespoon peanut oil
1 medium onion, diced
1 teaspoon freshly grated
  ginger
1 tablespoon peanut butter
1 tablespoon honey
Juice of 1 lemon
1 tablespoon cider vinegar
1½ pints (850ml) vegetable
  stock
¼ teaspoon cayenne pepper
Sea salt
Freshly ground black pepper

For the rice:
2 cups brown rice
4 cups water
2 tablespoons capers
Juice and finely julienned rind
  of 1 lemon

(Illustrated opposite.)

Broiled Vegetable Satay
with Lemon and Caper Rice

TOP AND TAIL each courgette and score the skins length-wise with a fork. Cut into 1-inch (2.5cm) pieces. Wash the mushrooms and trim if necessary. Peel and blanch the onions briefly. Rinse the tomatoes. Set the tomatoes aside, and thread the other vegetables onto 8 wooden skewers, alternating colours and textures.

Heat the oil in a pan and sauté the onion and ginger until softened. Then stir in all the other sauce ingredients and simmer until reduced by half.

Meanwhile, cook the rice by the pilaf method. Shortly before the rice is cooked, stir in the capers and lemon.

Baste the skewers with sauce and place in a baking dish in a medium oven (350°F/180°C/Gas Mark 4) for 12 minutes, turning and basting every few minutes. Shortly before serving, add a tomato to each end of each skewer and return to the oven to warm through.

Serve the skewers on a bed of rice, with extra sauce offered separately.

Note:
This is a substantial side dish that could be served as a light meal in itself, if wished.

1 lb (450g) baby carrots,
  scrubbed
Juice of 2 sweet oranges
2 cardamom pods, split
2 tablespoons brandy
1 tablespoon cornflour

Olive oil for frying
1 green pepper, seeded and
  diced
1 red pepper, seeded and diced
2 onions, chopped
2 cloves garlic, crushed
4 oz (100g) pine nuts
2 tomatoes, skinned and
  chopped
12 oz (350g) mushrooms,
  washed and quartered
1 teaspoon paprika
½ teaspoon cayenne pepper
4 cups cooked brown rice

Carrots in Orange and Brandy Sauce

COOK THE carrots in lightly salted boiling water to cover, until just tender. Meanwhile, reserve a little orange juice and heat the rest with the cardamom pods until simmering. Stir in the brandy and discard the cardamoms. Blend the cornflour with the reserved orange juice and thicken the sauce slightly with this. Simmer to cook the starch before draining the cooked carrots and glazing with sauce. Serve at once.

Spiced Rice

HEAT SOME olive oil in a large pan. Sauté the peppers, onion, garlic and pine nuts for about 2 minutes, then stir in the tomatoes, mushrooms and seasoning and cook for about 2 more minutes.

Stir in the cooked rice (adding a little more oil before this, if necessary) and sauté until heated through and starting to sizzle. Serve at once.

Steamed Mangetout, Celery and Spring Onions with Ginger and Orange

12 oz (350g) mangetout peas
4 oz (100g) celery
Small bunch spring onions
Piece of fresh ginger
Juice and finely julienned rind
    of ½ orange

TOP AND TAIL the mangetout peas. Trim the celery and cut into sticks about 2 inches (5cm) long, and the thickness of a pencil. Trim the spring onions (use more or less of these according to your taste for onion) and cut into 2-inch (5cm) lengths. Steam the vegetables together until tender. Serve at once, garnished with ginger and orange peel to your taste and dressed with a sprinkling of orange juice.

2 heads radicchio
4 oz (100g) mushrooms
1 tablespoon vegetable oil
1 cup cooked wild rice
Sea salt
Freshly ground black pepper
1 head soft lettuce
3 sticks celery
4 oz (100g) beansprouts
1 green pepper
Mayonnaise to bind

(Illustrated opposite.)

Two Leafy Parcels

WASH AND separate the leaves of radicchio. Drain well. Chop the mushrooms and sauté briefly in a little oil. Stir in the wild rice, season and leave the mixture to cool. Then use the radicchio leaves to make up 4 little parcels of the stuffing.

Separate the lettuce into leaves. Wash and drain well. Finely chop the celery, chop the beansprouts roughly, seed and dice the pepper and bind all these ingredients together with a little mayonnaise. Season to taste. Then use the lettuce leaves to make 4 little parcels of the filling.

Serve two parcels per portion, each on a leaf of the contrasting lettuce. Offer sauces that share the contrast of colours — such as one made of pink peppercorns and mustard, and the other a watercress sauce (see below).

Pink Peppercorn Mustard Sauce
Process together ¼ pint (150ml) mayonnaise, 2 tablespoons of pink peppercorns and 1 tablespoon of Dijon mustard or to taste.

Watercress Sauce
Blanch a trimmed bunch of watercress for 1 minute, then drain well and process with ¼ pint (150ml) mayonnaise and 1 tablespoon of chopped fresh mint.

Spinach Islands

8 perfect leaves spinach
1 cup cooked brown rice
2 finely chopped shallots
3 oz (75g) cooked red kidney
    beans
Freshly chopped mint
Finely grated lemon rind
Crushed garlic
Ground cumin
Cayenne pepper
Sea salt
Freshly ground black pepper
Toasted cashew nut halves, to
    garnish
Stoned black olives, to garnish

BLANCH THE spinach leaves briefly in boiling salted water. Lay out flat on kitchen paper to drain and cool.

In a bowl, mix together the rice, shallots and beans. Flavour with the rest of the ingredients (except the garnish) to your own taste. Lightly oil 4 elliptical baking moulds and line with spinach leaves, fill each one, and cover with the overhanging spinach to seal in the flavour.

Place the moulds in a bain marie and bake at 375°F/190°C (Gas Mark 5) for about 20 minutes.

Prepare a tomato sauce, such as that on page 56, and spoon a little onto each serving plate before turning out the spinach mould onto it. Garnish with nuts and olives, and serve at once.

Braised New Potatoes, Tomatoes and Shallots in Marmalade and Mint Sauce

1 lb (450g) peeled shallots
Vegetable oil
1 lb (450g) new potatoes,
    scrubbed
12 oz (350g) small sweet
    tomatoes
2 dessertspoons cider vinegar
3 tablespoons marmalade
Fresh mint leaves
Sea salt
Freshly ground black pepper
(Illustrated opposite.)

PLACE THE shallots in an ovenproof dish and add just enough oil to lightly coat them all over, but no more. Bake at 400°F/200°C (Gas Mark 6) for about 30 minutes.

Meanwhile, lightly boil or steam the potatoes. Take care not to overcook. Drain them if boiled and place in the baking dish that contains the shallots, together with the tomatoes. Stir in the cider vinegar and marmalade. Return the dish to the oven and cook for a further 20 minutes, stirring occasionally.

Check seasoning before serving, sprinkle with mint and serve straight from the dish.

Courgettes and Lentils, My Way

For the tomato demi-glace sauce:

2 tablespoons olive oil, for
    frying
1 onion, finely chopped
1 clove garlic, crushed
1 stick celery, finely chopped
1 carrot, finely chopped
8 oz (225g) fresh tomatoes,
    skinned and chopped
1 tablespoon tomato purée
Chopped fresh parsley
Pinch dried marjoram or
    mixed herbs
Freshly ground black pepper
Dão red wine

For the lentils:

4 oz (100g) lentils, soaked
1 onion, roughly chopped
1 clove garlic, chopped
Shoyu sauce, to taste
¼ pint (150ml) Dão red wine,
    approx.

For the bake:

12 oz (350g) courgettes
Olive oil, for frying
1 lb (450g) tomatoes, sliced
¼ pint (150ml) thick
    béchamel sauce, flavoured
    with mace

MAKE THE sauce by heating a little olive oil in a pan and sautéing the onion, garlic, celery and carrots until tender but not browned. Add the tomatoes and the tomato purée and cook gently so that the tomatoes are reduced to a pulp. Stir in herbs and seasoning, and add a little wine if the sauce is too thick. Set aside.

Drain the soaked lentils and place in a pan with the onion and garlic, and just enough water to cover. Cook until soft and season with shoyu. If the lentils get too dry while cooking, add red wine and some demi-glace sauce.

Slice the courgettes thinly and sauté briefly in a little olive oil. Place some in the base of a lightly-oiled ovenproof dish, then top with layers of sliced tomatoes, lentils, tomato sauce and béchamel sauce, finishing with a layer of béchamel.

Bake at 375°F/190°C (Gas Mark 5) until the mixture is bubbling. Serve at once.

Note:

This is another substantial side dish that could be served on its own for lunch or supper. If accompanying a large main course, it could also be made without the lentil layers, and still tastes very good indeed.

FINALIST I

Miranda Kennett

FIRST COURSE
Ogen and Cantaloupe Melon with Watercress and Roquefort Sauce
WINE: Gazela Vinho Verde

MAIN COURSE
Spinach Roulade with Red Onion and Ricotta Filling and Tomato Coulis
WINE: Gazela Dão Grão Vasco

SIDE DISH
Mushrooms in a Creamy Vermouth Sauce with a Hazelnut Crust
New Potatoes, French Beans

SALAD
Salad of Courgettes, Carrots and Nasturtium Flowers with Toasted Pumpkin Seeds, Basil and a Walnut Oil Dressing

CHEESES
Chèvre Cendré, Red Cheshire, Gorgonzola, Mascarpone, with Oatcakes
WINE: Gazela Dão Grão Vasco

PUDDING
Raspberry and Redcurrant Tartlets with a Honeyed Filling
WINE: Pink Champagne

Ogen and Cantaloupe Melon with Watercress and Roquefort Sauce

1 bunch watercress
3 oz (75g) Roquefort or Stilton cheese
1 egg
1 egg yolk
¼ pint (150ml) oil (see note)
Lemon juice
Freshly ground black pepper
½ ogen melon
½ cantaloupe melon
Sprigs of watercress, to garnish

WASH AND dry the watercress, and remove any coarse or damaged pieces. Place in a food processor with the cheese and blend to a smooth purée. Add the egg and the yolk and blend again. Now add the oil as for mayonnaise, by pouring down the feeder tube in a thin stream, with the motor running. Season with a squeeze of lemon juice and some black pepper. The sauce should be a delicate pale green, with the consistency of thin mayonnaise. Chill until required.

Remove the seeds from both melons, peel and slice thinly into crescents. Spoon a pool of sauce onto each of 4 serving plates and arrange alternate slices of orange and green melon over this. Decorate with sprigs of watercress.

Note:
For a flavoursome oil that does not drown the taste of the watercress, use one-third olive oil to two-thirds sunflower or grapeseed.

Spinach Roulade with Red Onion and Ricotta Filling and Tomato Coulis

For the roulade and filling:

1 oz (25g) butter
1 oz (25g) flour
¼ pint (150ml) milk
Sea salt
Freshly ground black pepper
Freshly grated nutmeg
Vegetable oil
7 oz (200g) cooked and drained spinach, chopped
4 large eggs, separated
1 tablespoon grated Gruyère cheese
1 tablespoon grated Parmesan cheese
6 oz (150g) Ricotta cheese
1 large red onion, finely chopped
Extra Parmesan, for garnish

For the tomato coulis:

12 oz (350g) tomatoes
1 large shallot, chopped
1 clove garlic, crushed
1 teaspoon olive oil
1 teaspoon tomato purée
¼ pint (150ml) vegetable stock
Pinch dried basil
Pinch dried thyme
1 bay leaf
Sea salt
Freshly ground black pepper

MAKE A thick white sauce with the butter, flour and milk. Cook gently for 20 minutes, stirring often and adding more milk if the sauce becomes too thick. Season with salt, pepper and nutmeg.

Heat the oven to 375°F/190°C (Gas Mark 5). Line a Swiss-roll tin with greaseproof paper and oil it lightly. Place the spinach, 1 tablespoon of the sauce, and the egg yolks in a blender or food processor. Season with salt, pepper and nutmeg, add the Gruyère, Parmesan and half the Ricotta. Process briefly to amalgamate. Stiffly beat the egg whites and fold them into the mixture. Spread the mixture as evenly as possible in the tin and bake for 15 to 20 minutes, until it is firm and lightly browned. Remove from the oven, cover with a clean tea-towel and turn it over onto a flat surface. Leave for 5 minutes before carefully peeling away the paper. If the edges are uneven, trim them.

While the roulade is cooking, make the tomato coulis. Skin and seed the tomatoes. Gently sauté the shallot and garlic in the oil until golden, then add the tomatoes, the tomato purée, the stock, and a generous pinch of thyme and basil and a bay leaf. Cover and cook gently for 20 minutes. Remove the bay leaf and purée the sauce. Check seasoning. If the sauce is too thin for your liking, return briefly to the pan to reduce.

Shortly before the roulade is cooked, add the onion to the remaining sauce and heat gently for 2 minutes. Stir in the rest of the Ricotta and cook for 3 minutes, thinning with a little more milk if necessary.

Spread the hot onion filling over the roulade, leaving the edges free for the filling to spread as you roll. With the long edge of the roulade towards you, use the tea-towel to help you roll the roulade into a Swiss-roll shape. You may find this easier if, before you start rolling, you make a small cut into both the short edges about 1 inch (2.5cm) from the edge you will start rolling with.

Transfer the roulade to a heated serving dish, so that the joint is underneath. Pour a little of the coulis down the centre of the roulade and scatter Parmesan over this. Serve at once, with the rest of the coulis in a separate bowl or jug.

Mushrooms in a Creamy Vermouth Sauce with a Hazelnut Crust

3 oz (75g) dried cèpes
8 oz (225g) field mushrooms
4 tablespoons sunflower oil
2 cloves garlic, crushed
1 tablespoon wholemeal flour
¼ pint (150ml) vegetable stock
2 tablespoons French dry vermouth
1 tablespoon shoyu
A good pinch dried thyme
2 tablespoons fromage blanc or cream
8 oz (225g) button mushrooms
4 oz (100g) hazelnuts
4 oz (100g) wholemeal breadcrumbs
Sea salt
Freshly ground black pepper

SOAK THE cèpes in warm water for 30 minutes. Wipe the field mushrooms and chop them finely in a food processor. Heat 1 tablespoon of oil and gently sauté the crushed garlic for 1 minute, then add the chopped mushrooms and cook for a further 2 minutes. Add the flour, stir well and cook for a further 2 minutes before stirring in the stock, vermouth, shoyu and thyme. Cook gently for 10 minutes, adding a little of the soaking liquid from the cèpes (strained first through muslin) if the mixture becomes too thick. Stir in the fromage blanc or cream. Set the sauce aside.

Wipe the button mushrooms and halve or quarter large ones. Sauté for a few minutes in 1 tablespoon of oil, then remove with a slotted spoon and place in a gratin dish. Drain and pat dry the cèpes and sauté in a tablespoon of oil. Add to the gratin dish. Pour the sauce over.

Mill the nuts coarsely and gently sauté them in the remaining oil with the breadcrumbs. Season well and add a little thyme. Spread over the dish and pat down lightly. Bake at 350°F/180°C (Gas Mark 4) for 20 to 25 minutes, when the top should be brown and firm. Serve at once.

Salad of Courgettes, Carrots and Nasturtium Flowers

For the dressing:
3 tablespoons walnut oil
1 teaspoon wholegrain
  mustard
1 teaspoon lemon juice
1 teaspoon fresh orange juice
Sea salt
Freshly ground black pepper

For the salad:
2 oz (50g) sunflower seeds
2 oz (50g) pumpkin seeds
8 oz (225g) young carrots
8 oz (225g) courgettes
8 nasturtium flowers
Fresh basil leaves

MIX ALL the dressing ingredients together in a screw top jar and set aside. Dry roast the seeds in a cast-iron pan until toasted but not burnt. Scrub and coarsely grate the carrots and courgettes. Toss in the dressing, along with the seeds. Divide between 4 salad bowls and decorate each one with 2 washed and dried nasturtium flowers and a sprinkling of basil leaves.

Raspberry and Redcurrant Tartlets with a Honeyed Filling

For the spiced pastry:
4 oz (100g) wholemeal flour
4 oz (100g) unbleached white flour
Pinch of mixed spice
2 tablespoons finely ground raw cane sugar
4 oz (100g) butter
1 egg
1 tablespoon vegetable oil

For the filling:
2 small punnets raspberries
2 tablespoons Armagnac or raspberry-flavoured Schnapps
1 punnet redcurrants
2 tablespoons honey
7 oz (200g) Quark
Icing sugar for decoration

COMBINE THE flours, spice, sugar and butter in the bowl of a food processor and mix for about 10 seconds. Add the egg and oil, beaten together, and mix for a few seconds to form a firm dough. Gather into a ball and place in a polythene bag. Leave in the fridge for 30 minutes.

Rinse the raspberries and marinate half of them in the liqueur for a few minutes while the redcurrants are washed and trimmed. Purée the marinated raspberries by pushing through a sieve. Chill.

Roll out the pastry as thin as possible and use it to line 6 fluted tartlet tins (the extra two are sure to be eaten up by appreciative guests!). Line with greaseproof paper and baking beans and bake blind for 15 to 20 minutes at 400°F/200°C (Gas Mark 6) until golden brown at the edges. Cool for a minute or two before removing from the tins to cool on a wire rack.

Beat the honey into the Quark and, when smooth, add the raspberry purée. When the pastry cases are quite cold, spoon in the chilled Quark mixture, decorate with whole raspberries and redcurrants, and finish with a dusting of icing sugar. Serve on individual plates, ideally on a bed of currant leaves.

SALADS

Cucumber, Nasturtium and Walnut Salad

For the salad:
1 cucumber
12 walnut kernels
12 nasturtium flowers

For the dressing:
1 tablespoon almond oil
1 tablespoon cider vinegar
4 freshly chopped mint leaves

DICE THE cucumber, chop the walnuts roughly, tear the nasturtium flowers into shreds and mix all together in a bowl, or arrange prettily on a platter. Place all the dressing ingredients in a screw top jar, shake well to blend and drizzle over the salad.

Avocado and Grapefruit Salad

SHRED THE lettuce. Wash the watercress well and remove tough stems and damaged pieces. Chop roughly. Lay the lettuce and watercress on a platter to form a bed for the salad. Divide the grapefruit into segments, using 1½ fruit for the salad, with the remainder being squeezed for juice. Slice the avocados and brush with grapefruit juice to prevent the slices from discolouring. Lay alternating segments of avocado and grapefruit onto the lettuce.

Place all the dressing ingredients, in a balance to suit your own taste, in a screw top jar and shake well to blend. Drizzle the dressing over the salad and serve at once.

For the salad:
1 head Webb's lettuce
1 bunch watercress
2 grapefruit
2 ripe avocados

For the dressing:
Olive oil
Grapefruit juice
Mustard of choice
Garlic, crushed
Pinch sugar
Freshly ground black pepper
Freshly chopped sage

French Mixed Salad

For the salad:
6 oz (150g) French beans
1 heart curly endive
1 small bunch oak leaf lettuce
Generous handful of rocket
    and watercress leaves

For the dressing:
1½ oz (45g) walnuts, finely
    chopped
4 tablespoons fruity olive oil
1 tablespoon cider vinegar
Sea salt
Freshly ground black pepper
1 teaspoon Meaux mustard

TOP AND TAIL the beans. Blanch in boiling water until just tender, then refresh under cold water and drain well. Rinse and drain all the salad leaves and place in a bowl together with the beans.

Whisk together all the dressing ingredients, pour over the salad, toss and serve at once.

Note:
Mangetout peas could be used instead of French beans, for variety.

Mint Cooler

6 oz (150g) courgettes
6 oz (150g) mangetout peas
4 oz (100g) black grapes
½ melon
Freshly chopped mint leaves
Natural yogurt

TOP AND TAIL the courgettes and slice them diagonally into very thin ovals. Slice the mangetouts into diagonal strips about ½ inch (1cm) wide. Halve and stone the grapes, and scoop the melon into balls. Toss the salad ingredients in a bowl with plenty of freshly chopped mint and refrigerate for several hours to allow the flavours to mingle.

Just before serving, pour over some natural yogurt and decorate with sprigs of mint.

Trans Salad

For the salad:
1 head curly endive
1 bunch watercress
1 avocado
½ cucumber

For the dressing:
2 teaspoons lemon juice
2 teaspoons olive oil
½ teaspoon chopped fresh
  tarragon
Sea salt
Freshly ground black pepper
Tiny pinch raw cane sugar

SEPARATE AND wash the endive leaves. Drain well and cut into strips. Wash the watercress well, removing any damaged leaves and coarse stalks. Divide into neat sprigs. Slice the avocado neatly and cut the cucumber into julienne sticks. Place all the salad ingredients in a bowl.

Place all the dressing ingredients in a screw top jar and shake well to blend. Pour over the salad, toss, and serve on individual plates.

Aegean Beans

1 lb (450g) tender French
   beans
1 large onion
8 oz (225g) ripe tomatoes
Sea salt
4 fl oz (120ml) olive oil
½ pint (300ml) boiling water
2 tablespoons shoyu

WASH, TOP and tail the beans. Cut into 2 inch (5cm) lengths and place them in a heavy-based saucepan. Peel the onion, slice in half and then into half-moons. Add to the pan. Peel and roughly chop the tomatoes and add to the pan. Sprinkle with sea salt and stir in the oil. Cover the pan with a lid and put onto a high heat. Cook for about 5 minutes, stirring occasionally.

Add the boiling water, bring to the boil, reduce the heat, season with shoyu and simmer the beans gently for 45 minutes.

Leave the beans to cool in the pan, still covered with a lid. Serve cold, but not chilled, on a large, flat serving plate of a light colour.

Note:
This is based on a dish eaten throughout Turkey as a vegetable dish or an accompaniment to cheese. Serve after your main course, first with some soft wholemeal bread, then introduce the cheeseboard and a selection of wholewheat crackers, allowing the cheeseboard to linger on a while after the salad has been finished.

For the salad:
2 oz (50g) cashew nuts
1 medium bulb fennel
2-inch (5cm) piece cucumber
2 oranges

For the dressing:
2 tablespoons sunflower oil
1-2 tablespoons orange juice
Sea salt
Freshly ground black pepper
Paprika

(Illustrated opposite.)

For the salad:
1 head escarole
1 bunch watercress
1 ripe pear

For the dressing:
Sunflower oil
Cider vinegar
Honey
A few walnuts
Sea salt

Fennel and Orange Salad

LIGHTLY TOAST the cashew nuts in a dry cast iron pan. Wash the fennel and trim, reserving any feathery leaves for a garnish. Chop the fennel finely. Dice the cucumber finely. Mix together the fennel, nuts and cucumber in a bowl.

Carefully segment the oranges, reserving any juice. Place all the dressing ingredients in a small bowl and mix well together. Pour over the fennel mixture and stir well to mix.

In 4 tulip shaped glasses, arrange layers of fennel mixture and orange segments. Garnish each glass with fennel fronds and a sprinkling of paprika. Chill well before serving.

Escarole, Watercress and Pear Salad with Walnut-Honey Dressing

RINSE AND drain the leaves of escarole, then tear them in two. Trim the watercress, wash and drain well, then separate into sprigs. Halve and core the pear and cut into thin 'fingers'. Place all the salad ingredients in a bowl.

Place all the dressing ingredients, in the quantity and balance of your choice, in a blender and reduce to a smooth, creamy dressing. Toss the salad with the dressing just before serving. The bitter-sweet tastes of the salad ingredients will remain distinct, while being united by the mellow flavour of the walnut dressing.

Countrywoman's Salad

For the dressing:
Olive oil
Freshly squeezed lime juice
Wine vinegar
Dijon mustard

For the salad:
Salad burnet
Lamb's lettuce
Dandelion leaves
Nasturtium leaves
Nasturtium flowers
Radicchio
Curly endive
French bread
1 clove garlic
Olive oil, for frying
Smoked tofu
Cider vinegar

PLACE THE ingredients for the vinaigrette, in the quantities and balance of your choice, into a screw-capped jar and shake well to blend.

Collect together your salad leaves and flowers in the quantities you choose or are able to obtain. Wash and drain them well and toss in the dressing. Arrange them on individual plates.

Toast slices of French bread on each side, then rub with garlic to make garlic croûtons. Place these on the plates.

Heat a little olive oil in a pan and lightly fry cubes of smoked tofu. Scatter the hot fried tofu over the salads. Add a dash of cider vinegar to the oil in the pan, mix well and pour over the salads. Serve at once to get the full effect of the hot and cold contrast.

Note:
This herb salad is very pretty to look at and delicious to eat. Smoked tofu adds protein to the dish, making it suitable as a main course salad if you wish.

FINALIST II

David Sowter

(Illustrated overleaf.)

FIRST COURSE
Pepper and Pear Compote
WINE: Gazela Vinho Verde

MAIN COURSE
Individual Artichoke and Asparagus Mousses in Cheese Sauce
WINE: Gazela Dão Grão Vasco

SIDE DISH
Fettucine Verde with Mushrooms, Hazelnuts and Pesto

SALAD
Chicory and Watercress Salad

CHEESES
West Country Cheddar, White Stilton and Dolcelatte
WINE: Hungarian Tokay Azsu

PUDDING
Stuffed Peaches
WINE: Hungarian Tokay Azsu

Pepper and Pear Compote

1 each of yellow, red and
white peppers (about
1 lb/450g total)
1 medium onion
1 glass Gazela Vinho Verde
white wine
1 pint (600ml) water
Peppercorns
Fresh herbs to taste
2 tablespoons extra virgin olive
oil
Freshly ground white pepper
1 large or 2 small avocado
pears
2 small dessert pears
1 pawpaw
Juice of 2 limes
A few kumquats
2 oz (50g) pickled ginger

WASH, TOP, tail and core the peppers. Slice lengthways into strips about 1 inch (2.5cm) wide. Cut the yellow and white peppers into lozenges and the red into thin 3 inch (7cm) strips.

Peel and coarsely chop the onion and simmer it for about 30 minutes with the wine, water, peppercorns and herbs. You could also use the trimmings from the peppers, but not too much of the red because the colour will stain the stock. When the stock is ready, strain through a fine sieve. Return to the pan and add the peppers (you may need to add a little more water to ensure the peppers are covered). Bring to the boil, simmer for 2 minutes, then drain the peppers and reserve the stock for the next recipe. Put the peppers on a shallow dish and dress with olive oil and white pepper while still warm. Leave to cool.

Quarter and peel the avocado pears and slice diagonally to form short strips. Peel and core one pear and cut into similar shapes. The other pear (preferably a soft-skinned one) should simply be cored and sliced thinly to garnish the border of the final dish. Halve, de-seed and peel the pawpaw and slice thinly lengthways. Dress the avocados, pears and pawpaw in lime juice and refrigerate until needed.

Wash the kumquats and immerse in boiling water for a few minutes, then plunge into cold water. Halve and remove their seeds.

To serve, make a border on each of 4 dishes using the pawpaw, pear slices and red pepper strips. Mix the yellow and white peppers with the avocado, the rest of the pears, and the rinsed and finely sliced ginger. Pile this mixture into the centre of the dish to contrast with the border. Serve at once.

Individual Artichoke and Asparagus Mousses with Cheese Sauce

For the mousses:
Perfect spinach leaves
8 tinned artichoke hearts
6 large eggs
¼ pint (150ml) double cream
Sea salt
Freshly ground black pepper
12 oz (350g) asparagus (approx. 20 spears)
Vegetable stock from cooking peppers (see page 102)
Vegetable oil for ramekins

For the vegetables and sauce:
8 oz (225g) trimmed leeks
8 oz (225g) French beans
¼ pint (150ml) vegetable stock
¼ pint (150ml) milk
Freshly ground nutmeg
Freshly ground white pepper
2 heaped teaspoons cornflour
3 oz (75g) grated Samsoe cheese
2 teaspoons drained capers

SELECT ENOUGH largish spinach leaves to cover a tea-towel, wash thoroughly, remove principal stalks and large veins. Blanch for a few seconds in a large pan of simmering water and drain out flat on the tea-towel.

Remove any discoloured leaves or darkened veins from the artichoke hearts. Liquidize with 4 of the eggs. Separate the other 2 eggs, add the yolks to the artichoke mixture and blend again. Stiffly beat the whites. Add the double cream to the artichoke purée and season to taste.

Prepare the asparagus by trimming and cutting into 3-inch (7cm) lengths. Blanch briefly in simmering water and then reserve 8 tips for garnish. Poach the rest in the vegetable stock for about 5 minutes or until just tender. Drain, reserving the stock, and allow to cool.

Lightly oil 4 largish ramekins and line with the spinach leaves, ensuring that enough overlap is allowed so that they can be completely covered during cooking. Fold the egg whites into the artichoke mixture and put 2 tablespoons of the mousse into each ramekin. Cover with a layer of asparagus pieces and fill with the rest of the artichoke mousse. Fold the spinach leaves over the top, then place in a bain marie and cover with any remaining spinach leaves. Bake at 375°F/190°C (Gas Mark 5) for about 30 minutes. (They can be kept warm in the bottom of a low oven for about another 15 minutes if necessary.)

While the ramekins are cooking, prepare the vegetables and sauce. Trim the leeks, removing the outer layers so that they are about ½-¾ inch (1-1.5cm) in diameter. Then cut into short lengths to make about 40 pieces. Reserve the trimmings for the cheese sauce. Top and tail the beans. Put the reserved asparagus tips in the vegetable stock and bring to the boil. After 1 minute add the leeks, then after a further 2 minutes add the beans. Cover and simmer for 2 minutes. Drain, reserving the stock to thin the sauce if necessary.

The sauce is made by bringing the milk to the boil with the leek trimmings, simmering for 10 minutes and then allowing to cool. Add 1 generous pinch each of nutmeg and white pepper, then liquidize. Thicken the sauce by beating the cornflour with a little cold milk, returning to the pan and bringing the liquid back to the boil. Just before serving, add the grated cheese and cook through. Blend again if necessary, make up to ½ pint (300ml) with stock, and stir in the capers.

To serve, discard the extra spinach leaves, run a knife around the ramekins and turn out a mousse towards one side of each warmed serving plate. Pour a little sauce over the mousse and over onto the uncovered part of the plate. Arrange the poached vegetables over this and place asparagus tips on top of each mousse. Serve the remaining sauce in a jug.

For the fettucine:
10 oz (300g) strong flour
2 oz (50g) cooked and drained
   spinach, chopped
1 dessertspoon olive oil
2 large eggs, beaten
Sea salt

For the pesto:
1 large handful basil leaves
2 oz (50g) hazelnuts
2 oz (50g) freshly grated
   Parmesan cheese
¼ pint (150ml) olive oil

For the sauce:
1 lb (450g) button mushrooms
2 tablespoons olive oil
2 oz (50g) coarsely chopped
   hazelnuts
3 fl oz (90ml) double cream
Sea salt
Freshly ground black pepper

Fettucine Verde

FIRST, MAKE the pasta by placing all the ingredients in a food processor and blending to a smooth dough. Leave to rest for 30 minutes before rolling out thinly and cutting into fettucine. Hang up to dry for a while before cooking.

Place the basil, hazelnuts and Parmesan in a processor and blend briefly. Then blend again, pouring olive oil down the feeder to make a mayonnaise-like cream. Set aside.

Wash and trim the mushrooms, then cut into slices just less than ¼ inch (5mm) thick. Heat the oil in a large pan and add half the mushrooms, stirring well to coat in oil. Cover and leave for 1 minute, then add the rest of the mushrooms, stir and cover again. After a minute they will have released some liquid. At this point, cook uncovered for a few minutes, then remove from the heat.

Meanwhile, bring a large pan of salted water to the boil and cook the pasta for a minute. Drain, add to the mushrooms, and return to the heat to finish cooking. Stir in the hazelnuts and the cream. Season to taste and reheat without boiling. Remove from the heat, swirl in the pesto and divide between 4 individual soup bowls.

8 oz (225g) small heads of
   chicory
1 large bunch watercress
1 handful flat parsley leaves
1 bunch spring onions
1 tablespoon sesame seed oil
1 tablespoon safflower oil
Juice of 1 lemon
Freshly ground white pepper

Chicory and Watercress Salad

SEPARATE THE leaves of chicory, then break each one in two lengthways by bending them by hand. Remove the leaves from the watercress (choose a large-leafed bunch if possible) and rinse in a colander with the parsley leaves. Trim and remove the outer layers from a bunch of spring onions. Split in two or four lengthways, and cut each so that strips are all about 3 inches (7cm) long, or about the same as the chicory strips.

Dress all the salad ingredients with the oils and refrigerate until needed. Just before serving, squeeze over the juice of a large lemon and a few twists of pepper. Serve at once.

Stuffed Peaches

4 very large or 8 small peaches
Lemon juice
2 egg whites
2 oz (50g) soft light brown
    sugar
2 oz (50g) ground almonds
1 oz (25g) butter
1 glass sweet white wine
1 lb (450g) strawberries
1 tablespoon soft raw cane
    sugar
Mint leaves to garnish

PLACE THE peaches in a large mixing bowl and pour on boiling water. Allow to stand for 10 minutes. Drain and cut the peaches in half, then remove the stones and slip the skins off. Sprinkle with lemon juice to prevent discolouration and allow to cool.

Beat the egg whites stiffly, then fold in the light brown sugar and the ground almonds. Place the peaches in a buttered ovenproof dish and pipe or spoon the almond mixture into the centre of each. Pour the sweet white wine into the bottom of the dish and place in the oven at 350°F/180°C (Gas Mark 4) for 30 minutes.

To prepare the sauce, first rinse and hull the strawberries. Reserve 8 for decoration and macerate the rest in the raw cane sugar for an hour. Then cook gently in a cast iron pan until soft. Pass through a sieve and return to the pan to reduce gently. When the peaches are cooked, pour the remaining wine from the baking dish into the strawberry pan. Keep the peaches warm while you further reduce the sauce until it is of spoon-coating thickness.

To serve, place two, three or four peach halves on each plate, stuffing-side up, drizzle with strawberry sauce and decorate with the reserved strawberries and fresh mint leaves.

DESSERTS AND PUDDINGS

Violet and Raspberry Fool

1 lb (450g) fresh raspberries
2 oz (50g) soft raw cane sugar
Handful crystallized violets
¾ pint (425ml) double cream, whipped
Extra raspberries and crystallized violets, for garnish

PLACE THE raspberries and sugar in a pan and stew together for a while to soften the fruit. Place in a food processor with the violets and purée together. Fold into the whipped cream.

Place a few fresh raspberries at the bottom of 4 serving glasses and spoon the fool over them. Decorate the top with crystallized violets and serve.

Raspberries with Minted Cream and Minted Chocolate

4 oz (100g) plain dessert chocolate
4 tablespoons crème de menthe liqueur
12 fl oz (350ml) double cream
2 tablespoons raw cane sugar
1 lb (450g) raspberries

(Illustrated opposite.)

HEAT THE chocolate and half the crème de menthe until runny. Do not boil. Mix well together and allow to cool slightly. Take very clean rose leaves and paint chocolate mixture onto the backs. Leave to set, then peel away the leaves to reveal chocolate ones. Chill.

Whip the cream with the remaining crème de menthe until it *just* holds its shape. Arrange the raspberries and cream in layers in tall glasses and top with chocolate leaves. Serve at once with a light, sweet dessert wine to drink.

Melon Fruit Bowl

1 large melon
About 12 oz (350g) fresh fruit
    of choice
Grand Marnier liqueur
½ pint (300ml) double cream,
    whipped
Dessert biscuits

CUT THE top third off a large melon. Discard the seeds, then scoop the flesh into small balls and place in a bowl. Prepare the fruit you have chosen and stir in with the melon balls. Sprinkle with Grand Marnier to taste.

Return the fruit to the melon shell and chill before serving with whipped cream and biscuits.

Note:
Choose soft fresh fruit such as strawberries, raspberries, stoned and diced plums or apricots, but let your choice be guided by what is at its best in the market on the morning of your meal. Serve glasses of Grand Marnier with dessert for a special meal.

Raspberry and Whisky Syllabub

1 lb (450g) fresh raspberries
4 tablespoons whisky
2 tablespoons clear honey
½ pint (300ml) double cream
¼ pint (150ml) natural yogurt
2 oz (50g) chopped roasted
    hazelnuts

PLACE MOST of the raspberries in a bowl, reserving a few for garnish. Pour over the whisky, stir in the honey and leave to marinate for several hours.

Drain the liquid off the raspberries into a jug. Pour ¼ pint (150ml) into a bowl, add the double cream and whisk until just stiff, then fold in the yogurt.

Put some marinated raspberries and a little of the left-over juice into 4 tall glasses. Cover with the syllabub mixture. Sprinkle with chopped hazelnuts and decorate with fresh raspberries.

Gooseberry Sorbet
with Orange Cream

For the sorbet:
1½ lb (680g) gooseberries
1 large glass Asti Spumante
¼ pint (150ml) water
6 oz (150g) sugar
1 egg white, stiffly beaten

For the orange cream:
½ pint (300ml) whipping
   cream
1 teaspoon frozen orange juice
½ teaspoon triple strength
   orange flower water
Approx. 2 teaspoons sugar

TOP AND TAIL the gooseberries and stew with the Asti until very tender. Purée in a blender and allow to cool.

Meanwhile, make a syrup of the water and sugar. Stir in the fruit purée and then freeze lightly. Remove from the freezer and fold in the beaten egg white. Freeze until set.

Lightly whip together the cream, orange juice and flower water with just enough sugar to taste. The mixture should be increased in volume but not stiff.

To serve, pour a pool of sauce onto each serving plate and top with a large scoop of sorbet.

Note:
Serve with almond and orange biscuits, made by following a standard almond tuile recipe with the addition of the grated rind of ½ an orange.

Berries Brulée

1 lb (450g) mixture of
   strawberries, raspberries and
   blackberries
2 tablespoons Cointreau
2 tablespoons strawberry
   liqueur
Juice of ½ a lemon
¼ pint (150ml) sour cream
¼ pint (150ml) natural yogurt
Muscovado sugar for topping

STEW THE fruit in the liqueurs and lemon juice for a maximum of 2 minutes, so that they are just softened. Divide between 4 ramekin dishes.

Whip together the cream and yogurt and spoon this mixture over the fruit, levelling the top. Heat the grill until very hot, then sprinkle sugar over the cream mixture to cover quite well. Place the ramekins under the grill until the sugar is lightly browned and caramelized. Serve at once with a good quality Liebfraumilch to complement the flavours.

2 ripe peaches
8 oz (225g) sugar
1 pint (600ml) water
8 oz (225g) raspberries
2 oz (50g) cyrstallized rose
  petals
2 tablespoons rosewater
3 stiffly beaten egg whites
Fresh borage flowers, to
  garnish
Sweet cecily, to garnish

Pêche Monroe

SKIN THE peaches, cut in half and remove the stones. Set aside.

Make a syrup of half the sugar and water. Add to this the raspberries and sieve to make a smooth purée. Set aside.

Make another batch of syrup with the rest of the sugar and water. Finely crush the rose petals and stir them into the syrup. Stir in the rosewater. Freeze to a mush, then fold in the stiffly beaten egg whites and re-freeze until firm.

To assemble the dish, pour a little raspberry purée onto each plate. Onto this lay a peach half that has been filled with sorbet. Decorate with borage flowers and fronds of cecily. Serve with a crisp, dry sparkling wine.

2 oz (50g) toasted pecan nuts
2 oz (50g) crushed digestive
  biscuits
½ pint (300ml) milk
2 oz (50g) butter
8 oz (225g) soft raw cane sugar
2 teaspoons powdered instant
  coffee
Whipped cream
Whole pecans, for garnish

Pecan Coffee Pots

CHOP THE pecan nuts and mix in a bowl with the crushed biscuits. Heat together in a pan the milk, butter, sugar and coffee, until the mixture is thick and fudge-like. Stir this into the bowl to bind the nuts and biscuits. Pour into individual ramekins and decorate with whipped cream and whole pecans. Serve with a glass of Bual Madeira to enhance the flavours of the nuts and the coffee.

Charlotte Louise with Chocolate Rose Leaves

15 sponge finger biscuits
2 oz (50g) redcurrant jelly
4 oz (100g) dessert chocolate
4 oz (100g) unsalted butter
4 oz (100g) ground almonds
2 oz (50g) castor sugar
¼ pint (150ml) double cream
A few drops natural vanilla
  essence
3 fl oz (90ml) sherry, brandy
  or whisky
Whipped cream, for
  decoration
Chocolate rose leaves (page
  109), for decoration

BRUSH THE base of a loose-based cake tin with a very little vegetable oil. Cut the biscuits in half, spread the sugared side with redcurrant jelly, then stand the biscuits neatly around the side of the tin to line completely.

Place the broken chocolate and the butter in a double boiler over a low heat and mix together once softened. Remove from the heat and stir in the almonds and sugar. Whip the cream stiffly and fold into the chocolate mixture. Stir in the vanilla essence and the alcohol. Spoon the mixture into the cake tin. Place in the fridge for at least 3 hours to chill and set.

Before serving, turn the charlotte out of the tin and decorate with whipped cream and chocolate rose leaves. Serve with pink champagne.

Stir-In Pudding

4 oz (110g) butter
4 oz (100g) castor sugar
2 eggs, beaten
6 oz (150g) self-raising flour
A little milk
12 oz (350g) gooseberries
1 oz (25g) butter

CREAM TOGETHER the butter and sugar, then beat in the eggs. Fold in the flour a little at a time. Add a little milk if necessary to give the mixture a smooth consistency. Top and tail the gooseberries, and stir them into the mixture.

Lightly butter a pudding basin and pour in the mixture. Cover with greaseproof paper and tie a pudding cloth over the top. Steam for 1½ hours. Turn out the pudding and serve at once with extra castor sugar, and clotted cream.

Note:
Bitter Morello cherries, stoned, could be used if gooseberries are unavailable. Raspberries would also be a good substitute.

Fresh Orange and Marmalade Flans

6 oz (150g) puff pastry
4 tablespoons marmalade
4 oranges

ROLL OUT the puff pastry and line four 4-inch (10cm) individual tartlet tins. Bake blind until golden brown at the edges and cooked through.

Use a little of the marmalade to glaze the base of the flans. Place the rest in a small pan.

Peel and segment the oranges. Arrange the segments in circles in each flan base. Heat the remaining marmalade until melted and pour this over the oranges. Leave to set at room temperature. Serve with home-made vanilla ice-cream to offset the tang of the oranges and marmalade, and to contrast with their vibrant colour.

Redcurrant and Almond Tart

6 oz (150g) rich shortcrust
    pastry
4 tablespoons redcurrant jelly
2 egg whites
2 tablespoons castor sugar
2 tablespoons ground almonds
8 oz (225g) fresh redcurrants
Toasted almonds
Small sprigs redcurrants, to
    garnish

(Illustrated opposite.)

ROLL OUT the pastry to line a flan tin, then bake blind. Warm the redcurrant jelly slightly and then spread the base of the pastry case with this. Beat the egg whites and sugar together until stiff, then fold in the ground almonds and trimmed redcurrants. Bake at 300°F/150°C (Gas Mark 2) until the meringue is browned, then serve sprinkled with toasted almonds and garnished with sprigs of redcurrants.

Blackcurrant and Cassis Cream

4 oz (100g) blackcurrants
4 tablespoons water
1 level tablespoon sugar
6 fl oz (180ml) thick set yogurt
6 fl oz (180ml) double cream
4 tablespoons crème de cassis
    liqueur

TOP AND TAIL the blackcurrants, then stew in the water until very soft. Stir in the sugar and then mash to a pulp or liquidize. Leave to cool, and then chill.

Beat together the yogurt and cream until thick. Fold in the chilled fruit purée to achieve a marbled effect. Spoon into individual glasses and chill before serving. Just before serving, spoon 1 tablespoon of cassis over each glass.

Lemon Pavlova with Summer Fruits

3 egg whites
6 oz (150g) castor sugar
Scant teaspoon white wine
 vinegar
Grated rind of 1 lemon
1 level dessertspoon cornflour
8 oz (225g) blackcurrants
Juice of ½ a lemon
2 oz (50g) raw cane sugar
8 oz (225g) raspberries
8 oz (225g) hulled strawberries
¼ pint (150ml) double cream

BEAT THE egg whites until very stiff. Gradually fold in the castor sugar, vinegar and lemon rind. Fold in the cornflour last. Rinse a baking sheet in cold water, then spoon the egg white onto this in a large circle. Preheat the oven to 400°F/200°C (Gas Mark 6) and put the baking sheet in, then immediately reduce the heat to 250°F/130°C (Gas Mark ½). Bake for 1¼ hours, undisturbed.

Top and tail the blackcurrants, then stew with the lemon juice and sugar until soft. Sieve and cool. Stir in the raspberries and strawberries.

Cool the cooked meringue. Whip the cream and spread this over it. Top with the fruit mixture. Refrigerate before serving. Serve in slices with a glass of Muscat de Beaumes-de-Venise.

Raspberry Cream Pie

⅓ pint (90ml) creamy milk
1 vanilla pod
3 egg yolks
3 oz (75g) castor sugar
1 lb (450g) fresh raspberries
Angelica, to garnish
Greek yogurt
Langues-de-Chat biscuits

HEAT THE milk very gently in a pan with the vanilla pod, until almost boiling. Beat together the egg yolks and one-third of the sugar until creamy. Remove the vanilla pod, then pour the milk over the eggs, beating well to mix.

Mix the raspberries with the remaining sugar and place in the base of a 1 pint (600ml) ovenproof glass dish. Strain the custard over them, shaking gently so that it settles amongst the fruit.

Place the dish in a bain marie and bake at 325°F/170°C (Gas Mark 3) for 35 to 40 minutes, until set. Cool for between 30 minutes and 1 hour, then turn out onto a green serving platter. Garnish with pieces of angelica and serve with Greek yogurt and biscuits.

FINALIST III

Lynn Walford

(Illustrated overleaf.)

FIRST COURSE

Chilled Asparagus Soup with Toasted Pine Kernels and served with Wholemeal Melba Toast topped with Lemon Butter

WINE: Gazela Vinho Verde

MAIN COURSE

Individual Crescents of Puff Pastry with Layers of Spinach and Wild Mushroom

WINE: Gazela Dão Grão Vasco

SIDE DISH

Individual Mousselines of Aubergine with Two Sauces - Coriander and Tomato

SALAD

Mixed Leaf Salad with Fresh Herb Dressing

CHEESES

Pont l'Evêque, Valençay, Bleu de Laqueille

PUDDING

Tulip of Fine Walnut Biscuit filled with Raspberry Parfait Topped with Fresh Peach Sautéed in Sauternes and Fresh Raspberries with Spun Sugar

WINE: Château de Malle 1979

Chilled Asparagus Soup with Toasted Pine Kernels

1 lb (450g) asparagus
3 shallots
1 oz (25g) butter
1¾ pints (1 litre) vegetable
    stock
¼ pint (150ml) cream
Squeezed parsley juice
Sea salt
Freshly ground black pepper
2 oz (50g) pine kernels
Wholemeal Melba toast, to
    serve
Lemon butter, to serve

TRIM AND chop the asparagus. Finely chop the shallots. Heat the butter in a pan and sweat the asparagus and shallots very gently until the shallots are softened. Then pour in the stock and simmer gently until the asparagus is tender. Purée in a blender or food processor, return to the pan and reheat with the cream, parsley juice for extra colour, and seasoning to taste. Do not allow to boil.

Toast the pine kernels in a dry cast-iron pan until just colouring. Serve the soup garnished with a sprinkling of these, and offer Melba toast and lemon butter to your guests.

Individual Crescents of Puff Pastry with Layers of Spinach and Wild Mushroom

8 oz (225g) puff pastry
1 lb (450g) fresh spinach,
    cooked and drained
Sea salt
Freshly ground black pepper
8 oz (225g) wild mushrooms
2 oz (50g) butter

ROLL OUT the flaky pastry thinly and cut into 12 crescent shapes. Bake at 425°F/220°C (Gas Mark 7) for about 15 minutes until risen and golden. Meanwhile, season the spinach well and heat with a little butter to keep warm. Clean and trim the mushrooms and sauté in butter until tender. Carefully layer the pastry crescents, first with a layer of tender cooked spinach, then a layer of wild mushrooms. Arrange on individual serving plates around the accompanying dish of Aubergine Mousseline (page 121).

Individual Mousselines of Aubergine with Two Sauces

For the mousselines:
2 aubergines
1 oz (25g) butter
1 shallot, chopped
2 eggs, beaten
½ pint (300ml) double cream

For the tomato sauce:
1 lb (450g) tomatoes, peeled,
    seeded and diced
1 oz (25g) butter
3 shallots, chopped
2 teaspoons tomato purée
Sea salt
Freshly ground black pepper

For the coriander sauce:
1 tablespoon crushed
    coriander seeds
2 shallots, chopped
1 oz (25g) butter
¼ pint (150ml) beurre blanc
    sauce

HEAT THE aubergines over a flame until the skin scorches and can be rubbed off. This improves the flavour of the aubergine. Chop the flesh and sauté in the butter with the chopped shallot until both are tender. Combine with the beaten eggs and cream then spoon into individual ramekins and place in a bain marie. Cover and steam until the mousselines are set and quite firm.

Sauté the tomatoes in the butter, with the chopped shallot until soft. Stir in tomato purée and let the sauce cook until thick. Season and keep warm.

Sauté the crushed coriander seeds and chopped shallot in butter until the shallot is tender. Stir in the beurre blanc sauce and simmer briefly. Strain, reheat and keep warm.

Run a sharp knife around the edge of the cooked mousseline. Place a spoonful of each sauce in the centre of each plate, turn out a mousseline onto this, and place a crescent of layered pastry on each side of the dish. Serve at once.

Mixed Leaf Salad
with Fresh Herb Dressing

Lamb's lettuce
Radicchio
Curly endive
Chicory
Nasturtium leaves
3 tablespoons walnut oil
1 tablespoon wine vinegar
Sea salt
Freshly ground black pepper
¼ teaspoon honey
Mixed herbs of choice, finely
   chopped

WASH AND drain a selection of salad leaves, such as those on the left, and arrange on individual serving plates. Place the oil, vinegar, seasoning, honey and herbs in a screw top jar and shake well to mix. Drizzle over the salad leaves and serve at once.

Tulip of Fine Walnut Biscuit filled with Raspberry Parfait and Topped with Fresh Peach in Sauternes

For the biscuits:
2 oz (50g) butter
4 oz (100g) castor sugar
2 oz (50g) flour
1 oz (25g) ground walnuts
½ teaspoon vanilla essence

For the peach:
1 peach
¼ pint (150ml) water
¼ pint (150ml) Sauternes
4 oz (100g) granulated sugar

For the parfait:
8 oz (225g) raspberries
¾ pint (350ml) thick Cornish cream
1 tablespoon chopped walnuts

MELT THE butter in a pan and stir in the sugar, allowing it to melt. Remove from the heat and beat in the flour, ground walnuts and vanilla essence. Put spoonfuls of the mixture onto a greased baking sheet, allowing plenty of room for spreading. Bake at 350°F/180°C (Gas Mark 4) for 8 to 10 minutes. Remove from the oven and allow to cool slightly before removing from the sheets with a palette knife and moulding into a fluted cup shape. Finish cooling on a wire rack.

Quarter and peel the peach. Make a syrup from the water, wine and sugar and poach the peach briefly in this, until just tender. Set aside to cool.

Purée and sieve the raspberries. Strain off a little of the Sauternes syrup and whisk it into the cream, along with the raspberry purée. Fold in the walnuts.

Place a biscuit tulip onto each serving plate. Spoon in some raspberry parfait and top with a quarter of peach. Decorate with extra fresh raspberries, and top with spun sugar for a truly special dessert.

RECIPE CREDITS

Soups

Carrot and Orange Soup	Verity Anne Meldrum
Red Wine and Lentil Soup	M van der Veen
Potage Crème de Piments	
Glacé au Gingembre	Ms K. E. Evennett
Chilled Cucumber Soup	J. P. & J. M. Holmes
Mangetout Soup	Mrs Maureen Jackson
Red Pepper and Coconut Soup	Roz Archer
Creamed Cashew Nut Soup	Philip Knott
Chilled Chick Pea and Lemon	
Soup	Maggie Schofield
Iced Herb Soup	Helen Clipsom

Starters

Avocado Terrine	Alison Leeming
Choux Puffs with Avocado	Leanne Dones
Individual Jalapeño Chilli Puffs	G. Jeter
Tomato Sorbet	Ms Helen J. Proops
Leek, Almond and Tarragon	
Custards with Red Pepper	
Chutney	Martin Yarnit
Individual Broccoli Soufflé	
Tartlets	Carla Shimeld
Watercress Roulade with Red	
Pepper Sauce	Mrs Helen K. Hallam
Fennel and Avocado Roulade	Sue Trevorrow

Main Courses

Buckwheat Crêpes Gâteau, layered with spinach and topped by a mushroom sauce	Mr P. E. Price

Gruyère Gougère with Leek, Mushroom and Caper Cream Sauce	Catheryn Lobbenberg
Légumes et Noisettes en Croûte	Ms Clare Conway
Individual Sweet Potato Soufflés	Cass Breen
Souffléed Potato Pancakes with Buttered Asparagus	Nancy Adshead
Spinach Rounds	Neil Fairlamb
Pastry Tarts with Three Fillings and Three Sauces	Jane Taylor
Savoury Rye Pancakes	Christine A. Horrocks
Onion Pasties with Tomato Sauce	George Tappenden
Tagliatelle with Brie Sauce	Carla Phillips
Poached Spinach Sausages	Emma F. Edgecombe
Saffron Gougère with Sorrel Sauce	Anne Decent
Fresh Lasagne Layered with Asparagus and Tomatoes and Mozzarella	Vicky Penrice
Silver Beet (Swiss Chard) Flan	Marie Archer
Petites Timbales Rayées, Sauce Beurre Blanc	Rosamond Richardson

Side Dishes

The Chef's Special Crunchy Rice	Ms N. R. Smith
Broiled Vegetable Satay with Lemon & Caper Rice	C. J. Lewis
Carrots in Orange and Brandy Sauce	Michael Millington
Spiced Rice	Judy van Es
Steamed Mangetout, Celery and Spring Onions with Ginger and Orange	Pam Windsor
Courgettes and Lentils, My Way	Katina Mendriros
Braised New Potatoes, Tomatoes and Shallots in Marmalade and Mint Sauce	Mrs A. Hudson
Two Leafy Parcels	Linda P. Piggott

Spinach Islands   Malcolm Ford

Salads
Cucumber, Nasturtium and
  Walnut Salad   Mitzi S. Cutler
Avocado and Grapefruit Salad   Lynne & Martin Grundy
French Mixed Salad   Brian Glover
Mint Cooler   Mrs Wendy Scaife
Trans Salad   Mrs I. Brooksbank
Aegean Beans   Sarah Carter Savaskan
Fennel and Orange Salad   Mrs S. Turner
Countrywoman's Salad   Alison Leeming
Escarole, Watercress and Pear
  Salad with Walnut-Honey
  Dressing   Melissa Key

Desserts and Puddings
Melon Fruit Bowl   Miss Marianne Geadah
Raspberry and Whisky
  Syllabub   Mrs Wendy Scaife
Violet and Raspberry Fool   Mitzi S. Cutler
Raspberries with Minted
  Cream and Minted
  Chocolate   Michael Millington
Fresh Orange and Marmalade
  Flans   C. J. Lewis
Redcurrant and Almond Tart   Patricia Scott
Blackcurrant and Cassis Cream   Christine A. Horrocks
Gooseberry Sorbet with
  Orange Cream   Roz Archer
Berries Brulée   G. Jeter
Pêche Monroe   Alison Leeming
Pecan Coffee Pots   Mrs Wendy Johnson
Charlotte Louise with
  Chocolate Rose Leaves   Verity Anne Meldrum
Stir-in Pudding   George Tappenden
Lemon Pavlova with Summer
  Fruits   Ms Clare Conway
Raspberry Cream Pie   Anne Decent

INDEX